The Green
Festival
Reader

The Green Festival Reader

Fresh Ideas from Agents of Change

Edited by
Kevin Danaher and **Alisa Gravitz**

Foreword by Medea Benjamin

PoliPointPress

The Green Festival Reader: Fresh Ideas from Agents of Change

Copyright © 2008 by Kevin Danaher and Alisa Gravitz

12 11 10 09 08   1 2 3 4 5

Production management: Michael Bass Associates
Book design: Andrea Reider
Cover design: Charles Kreloff Design

Library of Congress Cataloging-in-Publication Data has been applied for.

ISBN 978-0-979-4822-8-1

Published by:
PoliPointPress, LLC
P.O. Box 3008
Sausalito, CA 94966-3008
(415) 339-4100
p3books.com

Distributed by Ingram Publisher Services

Printed in the United States of America

Contents

Foreword

At a White House press briefing on May 7, 2001, Press Secretary Ari Fleischer was asked how the president would address the rising gas prices. "Given the amount of energy Americans consume per capita, how much it exceeds any other citizen in any other country in the world, does the president believe we need to correct our lifestyles to address the energy problem?" a reporter asked.

"That's a big no," Fleischer replied adamantly. "The president believes that it should be the goal of policymakers to protect the American way of life. The American way of life is a blessed one. . . . The president also believes that the American people's use of energy is a reflection of the strength of our economy, of the way of life that the American people have come to enjoy."

Just months before the fatal attack of September 11, 2001, America was living in a bubble. We celebrated Earth Day once a year, but the rest of the year we consumed to our heart's content. Our "blessed" way of life was destroying the planet.

The commodity that best embodied this "shop 'til you drop" worldview is the Hummer. First produced in 1992, this gas-guzzling, menacing vehicle has been the quintessential symbol of human arrogance against Mother Nature. The Hummer's dreadful 10 miles per gallon is less than half the mileage of the Model T Ford some 80 years ago! Hummers emit over three times more carbon dioxide than average cars, hastening global warming. Categorized as light trucks, they were exempt from emission or fuel-efficiency standards.

Hummer owners were also able to take advantage of a tax loophole originally meant to help farmers purchase tractors. The loophole allows tax write-offs for vehicles over 6,000 pounds, up to the cost of the vehicle. So those who bought this insane military-turned-civilian vehicle could get a $100,000 tax break!

Hummers became the ultimate status symbol of manliness. Bodybuilder Arnold Schwarzenegger, credited with promoting the civilian marketing of the military Humvee, had a whole fleet of them. Athletes, rappers, movie stars gobbled them up. By 2002, Hummers were in such demand that customers were waiting months to take delivery and were bidding above the sticker price. U.S. sales reached a peak of 71,524 in 2006.

For environmentalists and antiwar activists, the Hummer was our nemesis, symbolizing not only hyperconsumption but also the glorification of war. At auto shows around the country, our CODEPINK protesters would jump on top of the bright, shiny monsters and drape them in banners that read "Real soldiers are dying in their Hummers so you can play soldier in yours." We protested at dealerships; we slapped Hummers with "IN VIOLATION OF MOTHER EARTH" parking tickets or bumper stickers saying "BIG HUMMER, LITTLE D**K; we lobbied Congress to rescind the tax breaks. More radical environmental groups set Hummer dealerships on fire.

It was not the protests, however, but the meteoric rise in gas prices that led to the Hummer's demise. By 2008, with gas prices passing $4 a gallon, consumers recoiled at spending $125 to fill their tanks. Celebrities became embarrassed to be seen in their Hummers and jumped on the Prius bandwagon instead. Hummer sales were so miserable that in June 2008, General Motors announced plans for a radical makeover. "We're considering all options for the Hummer brand, from a complete revamp of the product lineup to a partial or complete sale of the brand," announced GM CEO Rick Wagoner.

It's not just Hummers that tanked. GM announced it was closing four assembly plants producing SUVs and pickup trucks. After years of polluting the roads with these oversized vehicles, GM said it would focus on smaller, more fuel-efficient cars, including a new plug-in hybrid and an electric car (after they sabotaged their own electric cars in the 1990s!).

The death of the Hummer marks the end of an era when flat-worlders mocked the concept of global warming and peak oil. It marks the end of an era when hyperconsumption was considered the God-given birthright of Americans.

But the old, fossil fuel–based economy will not die a quick death. A dying bull kicks the hardest, and the corporate dinosaurs that live off "big oil" are trying desperately to keep their stranglehold over our lives.

Automakers continue to drag their feet in producing truly fuel-efficient cars, while trapped consumers must still depend on cars due to the pitiful state of our public transportation system.

Our economy still runs on oil, and big oil continues to pollute the world's air, land, and water. Oil companies, making record profits, get massive subsidies from Congress, while oil executives buy off candidates with obscene amounts of campaign cash.

Our soldiers are still dying in Iraq so U.S. companies can appropriate Iraqi oil. Our government cozies up to the repressive monarchy in Saudi Arabia, supports drilling and killing in Nigeria, backs a coup against the democratically elected leader of oil-rich Venezuela, and pressures the OPEC drug pusher to pump more and more.

The military-industrial complex still reigns supreme, with more than 700 U.S. military bases around the world representing the old model of domination, militarism, and environmental contamination.

But as we see through this book and the Green Festivals (both co-produced by Global Exchange and Co-op America), the sprouting green economy is bursting through the hard steel shell of the Hummer economy. Communities are demanding bike lanes and reliable public transportation. Consumers are driving less, demanding efficient cars, and using mass transit more. Congress is getting rid of tax codes that favor gas guzzlers, funding research on fuel efficiency, and funding green jobs. The business world is retooling to offer innovative products that conserve energy and provide alternatives to fossil fuels. Cities are competing to see which one can pass the most forward-thinking, green initiatives.

Even on the seemingly intractable issue of the U.S. imperial reach, innovative visions are being proposed as long-term goals of reshaping our global footprint. In fact, it was at a Green Festival that Green Festival founder Kevin Danaher and I first put forth the idea of a campaign to transform the vast U.S. network of overseas military bases into ecodevelopment centers, producing solar panels, windmills, and other forms of alternative energy; promoting organic agriculture and permaculture; experimenting with green building technologies; and teaching practical skills needed to save humanity from itself.

The conversion of these bases into models of ecodevelopment would help transform the United States from a dominating empire into a global partner, thereby making us less of a target for terrorist attacks. It would save the United States billions of dollars now being wasted maintaining this global network of bases. It would create collaborative platforms for coalescing the diverse pieces of the green economy, and it would help countries implement more sustainable practices, thus helping to restore the natural systems we all rely on.

Such a vision of military–turned–green entrepreneur might seem like a pipedream, but who predicted that the Hummer would meet such a sudden demise? The next few decades will be marked by massive innovations as we desperately try to deal with the crises generated by our present economic model. This book, and the movement it describes, will give you ample fodder for rethinking our present predicament and playing a more active role in the global awakening.

Medea Benjamin
Cofounder of Global Exchange and
CODEPINK: Women for Peace

Introduction

KEVIN DANAHER AND ALISA GRAVITZ

> Power is the strength required to bring about social,
> political, and economic change. . . . Power at its
> best is love implementing the demands
> of justice, and justice at its best is love correcting
> everything that stands against love.
> —DR. MARTIN LUTHER KING JR.

A s Yankee catcher Yogi Berra once said, "When you come to a fork in the road, take it." The human race is now at a fork in the road. We can either continue destroying the environment, denying people their human rights, allowing social and economic injustice, fueling the inequality between the haves and have-nots, and threatening the very existence of our species—or we can create a green economy that meets human needs while not destroying other species.

Ironically, there is a positive side to the destruction of the environment. As the consequences of our nature-destroying economy become increasingly evident, it becomes harder for people to deny that we need to change our ways and adopt more sustainable practices. The public mind is being opened to the looming environmental crisis by the collapse of biological systems around the world: topsoil is being depleted, glaciers and the polar ice caps are melting, fresh water supplies are being poisoned and depleted, thousands of species of flora and fauna are going extinct, extreme weather events are causing increased casualties and property damage, ocean levels are rising from warmer temperatures, and the list could go on. These, and other signs that we humans are destroying the biological basis for our very existence, are causing more people to realize the urgency of a transition to conservation economics.

In addition to destroying the environment, our economic system perpetuates social and economic injustices. Our coal-fired power plants fuel a national asthma epidemic, harming all our children. Society dumps its toxic waste in neighborhoods where poor people live, both here and abroad. Our big-box "business model" destroys jobs and communities here, and creates a whole new generation of sweatshops with slave wages and horrible working conditions around the world to put cheap goods in the box stores.

That is why Co-op America and Global Exchange produce the Green Festivals. The events provide a space where forward-thinking people can come together to create synergies and realize we are all part of the same movement for change. The environmental crisis confronting the human race can be seen as a historic opportunity to create a totally new economic system that makes its money by healing nature, respecting people, and nurturing thriving local communities, rather than destroying them.

We call this a "festival" because it is a festive occasion. This is a party, but not as in a political party; this party is a verb, as in "Let's party." The conference portion of the event deals with some very weighty topics, so it is important for the rest of the event to be loaded with joy and exuberance. While nourishing the senses with great food, jumping music, family activities, yoga and movement classes, art and film, and lots of exciting exhibits of cutting-edge technology, we also feed the mind and soul with some of the most insightful speakers in the world.

The Green Festivals bring together the greenest thinkers and activists in all three sectors—government, nonprofit, and for-profit—because collaboration of all three is necessary to make the transition to the green economy. This strategy of networking is spreading. We are seeing movements creating resilient communities and going local with food systems, along with groups like BALLE (the Business Alliance for Local Living Economies), ICLEI, (the International Council of Local Environmental Initiatives), the Institute for Local Self Reliance, the Funders' Network on Smart Growth and Livable Communities, as well as our own organizations, Global Exchange and Co-op America, and many others that are building alliances that cross institutional and national boundaries. If you go to our website (greenfestivals.org), you can stream the audio and video recordings of our speakers, and you will see that they represent all three sectors.

These networks are united by a common goal of creating a different economic system: one that is democratically organized, heals the wounds of social inequality, and heals the environment; and all of this while making money and distributing the surplus evenly! As Tom Szaky, the cofounder of TerraCycle says: "I didn't start the company to save the environment; I started it to prove that you can make a lot of money saving the environment."

Remember how the right wing in the United States made *liberal* a dirty word? Well, we need to take *conservative* and redefine it as a positive word. What does it mean to conserve? To conserve means to respect nature's limits, to respect people's cultures and their human rights. To this end, the Green Festival is laying the foundation for what might be termed the "conservation economy."

The people in power are getting more defensive as the corporate model collapses around them. Defenders of the existing system say nutty things to justify the inequality of the profit-driven economic model. They say, "It is a rat race." But rats don't race! Or they say, "It's a dog-eat-dog world." But dogs don't eat dogs! Think about that: defenders of the system have to lie about rats and dogs in order to justify their system.

The corporate globalization project is failing. It is creating more inequality—within countries and across the planet—and it is destroying the environment. That is due to three deep-seated structural flaws in the most powerful institution of the system: the transnational corporation. It is not democratically organized, it is not rooted in place (no patriotism to any specific community), and it values money over nature and people.

The opposite of the transnational corporation is the local green economy movement. It is made up of many small institutions working collaboratively to democratize the way capital gets invested, it is very rooted in specific communities, and it understands the importance of making money by restoring nature rather than destroying it. It also recognizes and celebrates that we are interconnected globally, and it envisions local communities and businesses trading with each other around the world, with fair trading systems, nurturing and deepening everyone's community.

This movement is spawning some of the most original thinking and exciting technology ever known. The gap between what is and what could be is greater now than at any previous point in history. The amount of human energy that can be released jumping from what is to what could be will be greater than any energy from any other source.

The authors presented in this book are among the brightest beacons on the horizon, pointing the direction we need to take to save humanity from itself. They are also among the leaders who are developing practical strategies for how we can restructure our institutions and personal behavior to create a human society that is truly sustainable over the long term. These authors are activist intellectuals or intellectual activists: they marry the best of thought and action. They are involved in practical struggles to create more joy and less suffering in the world.

It is this kind of simple yet visionary thinking that we present in this book. We hope it will make you laugh, cry, and think critically—and then act to change the course of history.

Please enjoy this book. May it give you inspiration and ideas for all you do to create a more just, sustainable, compassionate future. And please join us at the Green Festivals to continue this feast of inspiration, ideas and joy.

> I believe that unarmed truth and unconditional love
> will have the final word in reality. . . . I have the audac-
> ity to believe that peoples everywhere can have three
> meals a day for their bodies, education and culture
> for their minds, and dignity, equality,
> and freedom for their spirits.
>
> —DR. MARTIN LUTHER KING JR.

PART ONE

The Global Crisis and a Prescription for Change

Confronting the Facts
of Climate Change

ROSS GELBSPAN

Formerly a special projects editor at the Boston Globe, *Ross Gelbspan conceived, directed, and edited a series of articles that won a Pulitzer Prize in 1984. His books include* The Heat Is On: The High Stakes Battle over Earth's Threatened Climate *and* Boiling Point: How Politicians, Big Oil and Coal, Journalists, and Activists Have Fueled the Climate Crisis— and What We Can Do to Avert Disaster.

The panic among climate scientists is expressing itself in geoengineering proposals that are half-baked, fantastically futuristic, and, in some cases, reckless. Put forth by otherwise sober and respected scientists, the schemes are intended to basically allow us to continue burning coal and oil.

Nobel laureate Paul Crutzen, for example, is proposing to spray aerosols into the upper atmosphere to reduce the amount of sunlight hitting the Earth. Tom M. L. Wigley, a highly esteemed climate scientist at the National Center for Atmospheric Research (NCAR), ran scenarios of stratospheric sulfate injection—on the

scale of the estimated 10 million tons of sulfur emitted when
Mount Pinatubo erupted in 1991—through supercomputer mod-
els of the climate, and reported that Crutzen's idea would, indeed,
seem to work. The scheme was highlighted in an op-ed in the
New York Times by Ken Caldeira, a climate researcher at the
Carnegie Institution.[1]

Unfortunately, the seeding of the atmosphere with sun-
reflecting particles could trigger a global drought, according to
a study by other researchers. "It is a Band-Aid fix that does not
work," said study coauthor Kevin Trenberth of NCAR. The
eruption of Pinatubo was followed by a significant drop-off of
rainfall over land and a record decrease in runoff and freshwater discharge into the ocean, according to a recently published
study by Trenberth and other scientists.[2]

The noted British ecologist James Lovelock recently proposed the idea of installing deepwater pipes on the ocean floor
to pump cold water to the surface to enhance the ocean's ability
to absorb carbon dioxide.[3] Others suggest dumping iron filings
into the ocean to increase the growth of algae, which, in turn,
would absorb more carbon dioxide.[4]

These proposals fail to seriously acknowledge the possibility of unanticipated impacts on ocean dynamics or marine
ecosystems or atmospheric conditions. We have no idea what
would result from efforts to geoengineer our way around nature's
roadblock.

At a recent conference, Lisa Speer of the Natural Resources
Defense Council noted, "These types of proposals are multiplying around the world, and there is no structure in place to eval-
uate if any of them work. People are going after these gigantic
projects without any thoughtful, rational process."[5]

What these scientists are offering us are technological expres-
sions of their own supercharged sense of desperation. To be fair,

the reality that faces us all is extremely difficult to deal with—as much from an existential as from a scientific point of view.

Climate change won't kill all of us, but it will dramatically reduce the human population through the warming-driven spread of infectious disease, the collapse of agriculture in traditionally fertile areas, and the increasing scarcity of fresh drinking water. Witness the 1-in-100-year drought in the southeastern United States, which has been threatening drinking water supplies in Georgia and other states.[6]

Those problems will be dramatically intensified by an influx of environmental refugees whose crops are destroyed by weather extremes or whose freshwater sources have dried up or whose homelands are going under from rising sea levels.[7]

In March 2007, the U.S. Army War College sponsored a conference on the security implications of climate change. "Climate change is a national security issue," retired General Gordon R. Sullivan, chair of the Military Advisory Board and former Army chief of staff, said in releasing a report that grew out of the conference. "[C]limate instability will lead to instability in geopolitics and impact American military operations around the world."[8]

One frequently overlooked potential casualty of accelerating climate change may be our tradition of democracy (corrupted as it already is). When governments have been confronted by breakdowns, they have frequently resorted to totalitarian measures to keep order in the face of chaos. It is not hard to imagine a state of emergency morphing into a much longer state of siege, especially since heat-trapping carbon dioxide stays in the atmosphere for about 100 years.

Add the escalating squeeze on our oil supplies, which could intensify our meanest instincts, and you have the ingredients for a long period of repression and conflict.

Ominously, this plays into the scenario explored by Naomi Klein in her book *The Shock Doctrine*—that the community of multinational corporations will seize on the coming catastrophes to elbow aside governments as agents of rescue and reconstruction, but only for communities that can afford to pay. This dark vision implies the increasing insulation of the world's wealthy minority from the rest of humanity, buying protection for their fortressed communities from the Halliburtons, Bechtels, and Blackwaters of the world while the majority of the poor are left to scramble for survival among the ruins.

The only antidote to that kind of future is a revitalization of government: an elevation of public mission above private interest and an end to the free market fundamentalism that has blinded much of the American public with its mindless belief in the divine power of markets. In short, it requires a revival of a system of participatory democracy that reflects our collective values far more accurately than the corporate state into which we have slid.

Unfortunately, we seem to be living in an age of historical amnesia. One wonders whether our institutional memory still recalls the impulses that gave rise to the Declaration of Independence and the U.S. Constitution, or whether we have substituted a belief in efficiency, economic rationalization, and profit maximization for our traditional pursuit of a finely calibrated balance between individual liberties and social justice.

To live without at least an open-ended sense of future (even if it's not an optimistic one) is to open one's self to a morass of conflicting impulses—from the anticipated thrill of a reckless plunge into hedonism to a profoundly demoralizing sense of hopelessness and a feeling that a lifelong guiding sense of purpose has suddenly evaporated.

This slow-motion collapse of the planet leaves us with the bitterest kind of awakening. For parents of young children, it provokes the most intimate kind of despair. For people whose happiness derives from a fulfilling sense of achievement in their work, this realization feels like a sudden, violent mugging. For those who feel a debt to all those past generations who worked so hard to create this civilization we have enjoyed, it feels like the ultimate trashing of history and tradition. For anyone anywhere who truly absorbs this reality and all that it implies, this realization leads into the deepest center of grief.

There needs to be another kind of thinking that centers neither on the profoundly dishonest denial promoted by the coal and oil industries, nor the misleading optimism of some environmentalists, nor the fatalistic indifference of the majority of people who just don't want to know.

There needs to be a vision that accommodates both the truth of the coming crisis and the profoundly human need for a sense of future.

That vision needs to be framed by the truly global nature of the problem. It starts with the recognition that this historical era of nationalism has become a stubborn, increasingly toxic impediment to our collective future. We all need to begin to think of ourselves, now, as citizens of one profoundly distressed planet.

I think that understanding involves a recognition that a clean environment is about far more than endangered species, toxic substances, and the "dead zones" that keep spreading off our shorelines. A clean environment is a basic human right. And without it, all the other human rights for which we have worked so hard will end up as grotesque caricatures of our deepest aspirations.

Fortunately, the timing of the climate crisis does coincide with other worldwide trends. Like it or not, the economy is becoming globalized. The globalization of communications now makes it possible for anyone to communicate with anyone else anywhere in the world. And, since it is no respecter of national boundaries, the global climate unites us as one race, the human race.

At the same time, the coming changes clearly suggest that, to the extent possible, we should be eating food from the local bioregion to minimize the carbon dioxide generated by factory farming and long-distance food transport. We should also be preparing to generate energy from a decentralized system using whichever noncarbon energy technologies are best suited to the bioregion: solar in sunny areas, offshore wave and tidal power in coastal areas, wind farms in the world's wind corridors, and geothermal almost everywhere. (It may even be feasible to maintain a low-level coal-fired grid, of about 15 percent of current capacity, as a backup for days the wind doesn't blow or the sun doesn't shine.) But it's critical to stop thinking in terms of centralized energy systems and to begin thinking in terms of localized, decentralized technologies. This makes sense for security reasons as well as environmental reasons: centralized energy production is a much easier target for those seeking to disrupt society, for whatever reason.

At the level of social organization, the coming changes imply the need to conduct something like 80 percent of our governance at the local grassroots level through some sort of consensual democratic process—with the remaining 20 percent conducted by representatives at the global level.

For some years, I have been promoting a policy bundle of three specific strategies as one model for jump-starting a global transition to clean energy. Those policies, which are spelled out in my book *Boiling Point* and on my website, include

- Redirecting more than $250 billion in subsidies in industrial countries away from coal and oil, and putting them behind carbon-free technologies;

- Creating a fund of about $300 billion a year for a decade, to transfer clean energy to poor countries; and
- Adopting within the Kyoto framework a mandatory progressive fossil-fuel efficiency standard that would go up by 5 percent a year until the 80 percent global reduction is attained.

The initial impulse behind these strategies was to craft a policy bundle to stabilize the climate—and at the same time create millions of jobs, especially in developing countries. Initially, I, along with the other people who helped formulate them, envisioned these solutions as a way to undermine the economic desperation that gives rise to so much anti-U.S. sentiment. They would, we hoped, turn impoverished and dependent countries into trading partners. They would raise living standards abroad without compromising ours. They would jump the renewable energy industry into a central driving engine of growth for the global economy and, ultimately, yield a far more equitable, more secure, and more prosperous world.

This kind of global public works plan, if initiated in the near term, could provide a platform to bring the people of the world together around a common global project that transcends traditional alliances and national antagonisms—even in today's profoundly fractured, degraded, and combative world. Along the way, it could also provide decentralized stand-alone energy sources for disconnected social communities in a postcrash world.

The key to our survival as a civil species during an era of profound natural upheaval lies in an enhanced sense of community. If we maintain the fiction that we can thrive as isolated individuals, we will find ourselves at the same emotional dead end as the current crop of survivalists: an existence marked by defensiveness, mistrust, suspicion, and fear.

As nature washes away our resources, overwhelms our infra-structures, and splinters our political alignments, our survival will depend increasingly on our willingness to join together as a global community. As the former Argentine climate negotiator, Raul Estrada-Oyuela, said, "We are all adrift in the same boat—and there's no way half the boat is going to sink."[9]

To keep ourselves afloat, we need to change the economic and political structures that determine how we behave. In this case, we need to elevate the ethic of cooperation over the deeply ingrained reflex of competition. We need to elevate our biolog-ical similarities over our geographic differences. We need, in the face of this oncoming onslaught, to reorganize our social struc-tures to reflect our most humane collective aspirations.

There is no body of expertise—no authoritative answers—for the challenge confronting us. We are crossing a threshold into uncharted territory. And since there is no precedent to guide us, we are left with only our own hearts to consult, what-ever courage we can muster, our instinctive dedication to a human future, and the intellectual integrity to look reality in the eye.

Notes

1. "How to Cool the Globe," Ken Caldeira, *New York Times*, op-ed page, October 24, 2007.

2. "'Volcano Cure' for Warming? Not So Fast, Study Says," *National Geographic News*, August 17, 2007.

3. "Lovelock Urges Ocean Climate Fix," *BBCnews.com*, Septem-ber 27, 2007.

4. "Seeds of a Solution—Could Iron Dropped in the Ocean Com-bat Climate Change?" *Boston Globe*, October 1, 2007.

5. Ibid.

6. "Drought-Stricken South Facing Tough Choices," *New York Times*, October 16, 2007.

7. "Military Sharpens Focus on Climate Change—A Decline in Resources Is Projected to Cause Increasing Instability Overseas," *Washington Post*, April 15, 2007.

8. "Climate Change Poses Serious Threat to U.S. National Security: New Report from Blue-Ribbon Panel of Senior Admirals and Generals Identifies Climate-Related Military Impacts," press release from the Military Advisory Board, April 15, 2007.

9. Raul Estrada-Oyuela, Argentine negotiator, at the UN Convention on Climate Change in Kyoto, Japan, December 1997.

The Great Turning

DAVID KORTEN

David Korten is cofounder and board chair of YES *magazine and the author of paradigm-shifting books such as* When Corporations Rule the World *and* The Great Turning: From Empire to Earth Community.

The day of reckoning has arrived. Global warming, the end of cheap oil, the exhaustion of fresh water, pending financial collapse, spreading social disintegration, all of these are manifestations of the monumental imbalances that we humans have created in our relations with one another and with the Earth. The choices we make at this defining moment will determine whether the inevitable correction plays out as a suicidal last-man-standing competition for what remains of the Earth's resources, or as a cooperative sharing of those resources to secure the health of our children, families, communities, and natural systems.

My book *The Great Turning: From Empire to Earth Community* begins with these prophetic words from the Earth Charter: "We stand at a defining moment in Earth's history, a time when humanity must choose its future. To move forward we must recognize that amidst a vast diversity of cultures and life forms, we are one human family and one Earth community with a common destiny." This is where the term *Earth community* comes from. The choice before us is actually between two contrasting models for organizing human affairs. One is the dominator model of Empire; the other is the partnership model of Earth community. We humans are likely to squander valuable time and resources on efforts to preserve or mend dominator cultures and institutions that cannot be fixed and must ultimately be replaced.

According to cultural historian Riane Eisler, our contemporary problem began some 5,000 years ago when our ancestors put aside the more egalitarian and gender-balanced ways of many earlier human societies and made a tragic turn from the partnership relations of Earth community to the dominator relations of Empire. As the transition played out, male gods replaced female gods. We humans lost our attachment to the Earth as the masculine drove out the feminine. Men took over, to rule by the sword. As conquest became the measure of human greatness, our societies became divided between the rulers and the ruled. Women and people of color were eliminated from the competition for power, simply by denying their humanity.

Every empire in history has exhibited three characteristics: First, empire reduces the majority of humans to conditions of depravation and servitude that deny their rights and suppress their creative potential. Every empire in our history, including our own, has been built on a foundation of slavery or its equivalent. Second, Empire diverts a major portion of the resources available to human societies away from meeting the needs of people and nature in order to support the military forces, prisons, palaces, temples, retainers, and propaganda that are required to secure the interests of an elite class against the wrath of those that bare the burden. Third, the institutions of Empire elevate the most power-hungry and ethically challenged among us to the highest positions of power.

Until we turn from the domination of Empire to the partnership of Earth community, there will be no end to patriarchy, racism, violence, exclusion, and environmental destruction. At the deepest level, many of our progressive causes are in fact one cause, and to succeed, we must recognize this unifying truth.

My concern is with publicly traded, limited liability corporations as institutions in which money has more protection than people and nature. Employees are required to abandon their personal values and are subject to instant, arbitrary dismissal. Decisions are directed exclusively to serving the short-term financial interests of absentee owners without regard to human or natural consequences.

The institutional infrastructure of global corporate Empire is destined to be stretched to its limits by the mounting forces of a perfect economic storm borne of a convergence of peak oil, climate change, and a meltdown of the U.S. dollar. Some experts believe that oil output may have already peaked; others predict it may not peak for another 20 or 30 years. But that difference is irrelevant. The era of cheap oil is over.

The challenge before us is how to turn a human crisis into a human opportunity. Here is the key: remove the environmental and social subsidies that prop up the global suicide economy, and it will bring the mother of all market corrections. The communities with the best prospect to weather the storm will be those that act now to rebuild local supply chains; reverse the trend toward conversion of farm and forest lands; concentrate population in compact communities that bring home, work, and recreation in easy reach by foot, bicycle, and public transportation; support local low-input family farms; and seek to become substantially self-reliant in food and energy.

Millions of people around the world are already working to turn this imperative into an opportunity to rebuild functioning communities, restore a sense of place, democratize economic power, and radically revise our priorities for the use of labor, land, and other natural resources in order to create societies that dramatically increase the quality of our lives, even as the quantity of our consumption declines.

The metamorphosis of the caterpillar to the butterfly, as told by evolution biologist Elisabet Sahtouris, is a very helpful metaphor for the turning from Empire to Earth community. The caterpillar is a voracious consumer that devotes its life to gorging on nature's bounty. When it has had its fill, it fastens itself to a twig and wraps itself in a chrysalis. Once snug inside, crisis strikes, as the structures of its cellular tissue begin to dissolve into an organic soup. This development represents disaster from the perspective of the caterpillar's lower worm nature but represents opportunity from the perspective of its higher butterfly nature. Guided by some deeper inner wisdom, a number of what scientists call "organizer cells" begin to rush around gathering other cells into multicellular structures that begin to form the crucial organs of a new creature.

Correctly perceiving a threat to the old order, the caterpillar's still-intact immune system attacks the organizer cells as alien intruders. The organizer cells prevail by linking with one another in a cooperative emergent process that gives birth to a new creature of extraordinary beauty that lives lightly on the Earth and serves the regeneration of life by pollinating plants. It has the capacity to traverse vast expanses. It experiences life's possibilities in ways the earthbound caterpillar could scarcely have imagined.

As our familiar institutional structures disintegrate around us, we stand on the threshold of a rebirth no less dramatic. Our transformation, if we are successful, will be cultural and spiritual. Our success depends on exercising our human capacity for conscious creative choice.

Unfortunately, our ability as a society to make the obvious choice for life is seriously hampered by the work of a small group of political extremists who claim to be conservative defenders of family values, but they cut programs that benefit children, families, communities, and nature in order to finance tax cuts for the rich, subsidies to crony corporations, and wars of imperial domination. These acts, as it turns out, are wholly at odds with what most Americans consider to be conservative values. The extremists behind this tragedy effectively hijacked the term *conservative*, and they hijacked both the Republican and Democratic parties to take control of our country.

We must take our country back. To do so, we must understand how they took control. Humans live by the stories that define our understanding of our relationships with one another and creation. In our society, the storytelling function has been taken over by propagandists and advertisers who have created a cultural trance that blinds us to our higher possibilities. This plays out in the prevailing stories that define the public discourse on prosperity, security, and meaning.

The imperial prosperity story tells us that economic growth fills our lives with limitless material abundance, lifts the poor from their misery, and creates the wealth necessary to protect the environment for the greater good of all. End poverty, not by taxing the rich but by eliminating welfare programs that create poverty by stripping the poor of their motivation to become productive members of society, willing to work hard at whatever jobs the market offers.

Here's the reality behind the imperial prosperity story. Modern societies define human progress by economic growth. By this measure, we have enjoyed enormous economic success. Just since 1970, global economic consumption has tripled, which has made a great deal of money for a few people, but at what cost?

The Living Planet Index, which is an index of the health of the planetary life support system, has declined by 30 percent since 1970, which means despite what GDP (gross domestic product) growth is telling us, we are growing ever poorer. If there is no life support system, there is no life. If there is no life, the whole concept of wealth loses any meaning.

The economic challenge before us is not to grow our economies; it is to reallocate our use of the Earth's resources to reduce destructive uses, increase beneficial uses, and give priority to those people most in need. We have a great deal of opportunity for reallocation. We can reallocate from military expenditures to health care and environmental rejuvenation, from automobiles to public transportation, from investing in suburban sprawl to investing in compact communities and reclaiming our forests and agricultural land, and from financial speculation to local entrepreneurship. We can reallocate from advertising to education.

Earth community has its own prosperity, security, and meaning stories that emphasize our connection to the Earth and affirm what we know in our hearts to be true. The Earth community prosperity story teaches that healthy children, families, communities, and living systems are the true measure of real wealth. They teach that mutual caring is the primary currency of healthy families and communities, that we increase real wealth when we invest in growing social capital and caring relationships and the natural capital of healthy ecosystems. They recognize that markets have an essential role in any vital community but that markets must have rules to secure community interests and maintain equity.

Earth community also has its security story, which teaches that exploitation and violence are indicators of failed relationships, that retribution against wrongdoers perpetuates violence, that healing troubled relationships eliminates the cause of violence, and that strong caring communities are an essential foundation of true security because they build trust, share risks, and create resilience when faced with crisis.

The Earth community story celebrates the integral spiritual intelligence from which all being is manifest. This story teaches that life is fundamentally a cooperative enterprise engaged in an unending search for unrealized possibility. It teaches that the species that survive and prosper over the long term are not the most brutal and aggressive. Rather, they are the species that find their place of service to the whole. True meaning is found through discovering and cultivating our human gift of service, as cocreators in a conscious, self-organizing cosmos.

We humans now face our final exam to determine whether we are a species worthy of survival. A passing grade will require a sweeping cultural and institutional transformation. Imperial stories teach us to believe that economic inequality is essential to progress, that the use of physical force is essential to social order, and that wealth and power are measures of righteousness. By contrast, Earth community stories teach reverence for the beauty and grandeur of creation. They call us to act as responsible adults, affirming our capacity to form authentic relationships grounded in love and mutual caring.

Although it may seem simple, to change the human course we must change the stories that define the culture. We must find the courage to break the silence so we can reach out to end our isolation by joining with others to grow authentic communities grounded in the principles of partnership. As we find our common voice, we will change the prevailing cultural stories, end the cultural trance, liberate the higher orders of human consciousness, and change the course of history.

Millions of people around the world are experiencing an awakening to the possibility of berthing a new human era grounded in principles of Earth community that transcends traditional human barriers of race, religion, and nationality. This awakening is manifest most visibly in a newly emergent social phenomenon called global civil society, a self-organizing, planetary-scale social organism that now functions as a shared conscience of the species. On February 15, 2003, it brought well over 10 million people to the streets of the world's cities and towns to oppose the violence of the planned U.S. invasion of Iraq. This was accomplished without the benefit of a central organization, an organizing budget, or a charismatic leader. It was all self-organized by millions of people acting on shared values, a social phenomenon unprecedented in human experience.

How could we possibly hope to build a consensus commitment to Earth community in our politically divided nation? Here's a hopeful truth: For all the talk of red states and blue states, polling data indicates that we are actually purple, and we have substantial agreement on many of the key issues. For example, 72 percent of us agree that big companies have too much power; 83 percent of us believe that as a society, the United States is focused on the wrong priorities; more than 80 percent want to give higher priority to the needs of children, family, community, and the natural environment. In other words, Americans want a world that puts people ahead of profits, spiritual values ahead of financial values, and international cooperation ahead of international domination.

This is a defining moment. We face a choice: either give up the reckless ways of our species adolescence and accept

responsibility for one another and the Earth, or continue on a
path to collective suicide. The spiritual force of creation is calling us to take the step to a new level of species maturity and to
find our place of service in the larger scheme of creation. We
wait at our peril for the leadership for this great work to come
from within the institutions of empire, global corporations,
national governments, and national political parties. They were
created as institutions of Empire to serve Empire.

Leadership in the Great Turning must come from people
like us, acting as the organizer cells of a new era, working from
the bottom up through our local governments, businesses, local
churches, educational institutions, and civic organizations to
build the vital democratic communities that will serve as the
imaginal buds of a new human era. Wherever we live, we must
each engage the challenge of making our particular community
of place an inspiring model for what can be for the nation and
the world, supporting one another as we break the silence, end
the isolation, change the story, and turn this world around.

Our distinctive human capacity for reflection and choice
carries a moral responsibility to care for one another and the
planet. In these turbulent, often frightening times, we must regularly remind ourselves that we are privileged to live at the most
exciting, creative moment of opportunity in the whole of the
human experience, because the future is in our hands. Now is
the hour. We have the power to turn this world around. We are
the ones we have been waiting for.

Nuclear Power? Forget about It!

Currently we draw electric power from about 400 nuclear plants worldwide. Nuclear proponents say we would have to scale up to around 17,000 nuclear plants to offset enough fossil fuels to begin making a dent in climate change. This isn't possible—neither are 2,500 or 3,000 more nuclear plants that many people frightened about climate change suggest. Here's why:

1. Nuclear waste. The waste from nuclear power plants will be toxic for humans for more than 100,000 years. It's untenable now to secure and store all of the waste from the plants that exist. To scale up to 2,500 or 3,000, let alone 17,000, plants is unthinkable.

2. Nuclear proliferation. In discussing the nuclear proliferation issue, Al Gore said, "During my eight years in the White House, every nuclear weapons proliferation issue we dealt with was connected to a nuclear reactor program." We can't develop a domestic nuclear energy program without confronting proliferation in other countries.

3. National security. Nuclear reactors represent a clear national security risk and an attractive target for terrorists. In researching the security around nuclear power plants, Robert Kennedy Jr. found that there are at least eight relatively easy ways to cause a major meltdown at a nuclear power plant.

4. Accidents. Forget terrorism for a moment, and remember that mere accidents—human error or natural disasters—can wreak just as much havoc at a nuclear power plant site. The Chernobyl disaster forced the evacuation and resettlement of nearly 400,000 people, without thousands poisoned by radiation. And nuclear power is unique in that one accident can scare off investment and halt the development of all new sites.

5. Cancer. There are growing concerns that living near nuclear plants increases the risk for childhood leukemia and other forms of cancer—even when a plant has an accident-free track record. One Texas study found increased cancer rates in north-central Texas since the Comanche Peak nuclear power plant was established in 1990, and a recent German study found childhood leukemia clusters near several nuclear power sites in Europe.

6. Not enough sites. Scaling up to 17,000—or 2,500 or 3,000—nuclear plants isn't possible simply due to the limitation of feasible sites. Nuclear plants need to be located near a large and dependable source of water for cooling, and there aren't enough locations in the world that are safe from droughts, flooding, hurricanes, earthquakes, or other potential disasters that could trigger a nuclear accident. Over 24 nuclear plants are at risk of needing to be shut down this year because of the drought in the Southeast. No water, no nuclear power.

7. Not enough uranium. Even if we could find enough feasible sites for a new generation of nuclear plants, we're running out of the uranium necessary to power them. Scientists in both the United States and United Kingdom have shown that if the current level of nuclear power were expanded to provide all the world's electricity, our uranium would be depleted in less than 10 years.

8. Costs. Some types of energy production, such as solar power, experience decreasing costs to scale—as do, say, computers and cell phones. When you make more solar panels, costs come down. Nuclear power, however, will experience increasing costs to scale. Due to dwindling sites and uranium resources, each successive new nuclear power plant will only see its costs rise, with taxpayers and consumers ultimately paying the price.

9. Private sector unwilling to finance. Due to all of the preceding points, the private sector has largely chosen to take a pass on the financial risks of nuclear power, which is what led the industry to seek corporate welfare from the government in the first place.

And finally, even if all of the above strikes against nuclear power didn't exist, nuclear power still can't be a climate solution because there is . . .

10. No time. Even if nuclear waste, proliferation, national security, accidents, cancer, and other dangers of uranium mining and transport, lack of sites, increasing costs, and a private sector unwilling to insure and finance the projects weren't enough to put an end to the debate of nuclear power as a solution for climate change, the final nail in nuclear's coffin is time. We have the next 10 years to mount a global effort against climate change. It simply isn't possible to build 17,000—or 2,500, or 17, for that matter—in 10 years.

With so many strikes against nuclear power, it should be off the table as a climate solution, and we need to turn our energies toward the technologies and strategies that can truly make a difference: solar power, wind power, lunar power (tides and waves), and energy conservation.

PART TWO

Challenging
Business as Usual

We Need a
Green New Deal

DENNIS KUCINICH

Dennis Kucinich, the former mayor of Cleveland, Ohio, is a Democratic representative in Congress from the 10th District of Ohio. Most recently, he was a Democratic candidate for president of the United States.

When we come to understand the interconnection between ourselves and nature, we understand the deep meaning of Thomas Berry's message; he wrote that "the great work" we have in this world is to restore our relationship to nature and understand how we all must come together in this common effort to save our planet and save ourselves.

We need a plan of green action—a Green New Deal—that will come about only if we have the courage to make some really tough political changes. Our current world trading system is in need of major reform. We need to cancel the North American Free Trade Agreement (NAFTA) and the World Trade Organization (WTO) and go back to bilateral trade based on criteria of social justice and environmental restoration. We must insist that all of our trade agreements protect the air and the water and the workers who produce the products we consume.

The WTO has ruled that the attempt to impose environmental principles in trade agreements constitutes a barrier to trade. Therefore, the WTO constitutes a barrier to sustainability, and we must change it.

If we base commerce on principles of sustainability, then commerce can repair the world. That ought to be a principle carefully enshrined in our economic treaties. Our trading relationship with China has not been wise in not having some conditions that we ask China to observe with respect to the environment. I met with the Chinese minister at the World Summit on Sustainability in Johannesburg a few years ago, and we were discussing how China was moving toward building coal-fired power plants, nuclear plants, and damming up huge rivers to create hydroelectric projects. When I questioned him about the path China was choosing, he responded by saying, "Mr. Congressman, we are still riding around on bicycles in our country," and my response was "That is a pretty good idea." In Amsterdam, everyone rides bicycles, and no one considers Holland a backward country—quite the opposite. We need to engage China in a constructive way, so that huge economic engine can present them with better choices that are more sustainable for China and the planet.

We understand our responsibility as the primary producer of greenhouse gases, to get our own house in order, so we have the kind of credibility that would cause other nations to say, "Well, you are moving in the direction of sustainability, and so, therefore the United States has credibility and others will follow." That has to be an underlying principle of our green policies internationally. We have to clean up our own house first.

When it comes to the greening of agriculture, we know that agribusiness has taken a direction that is against the interests of the land, the water, and the family farmers. We need sustainable agricultural policies that implement the precautionary principle: companies cannot deploy biotechnology until it is proven to be safe. All genetically modified organisms should be tested for allergenicity and toxicity to make sure that all genetically modified organisms are labeled to make sure that consumers and organic farmers are protected. Sustainable agricultural practices can become a basis for saving the land and saving the planet.

Our agricultural policies also need to promote the wise use of water, which currently constitutes one of our greatest endangered resources in the world. In Iowa, I learned of the confined animal feeding operations, which are poisoning the water table in Iowa and a number of other states. A Green New Deal means not confining these animals to where they have no room to breathe. It means to make sure that we realize our connection to all of God's creatures.

A Green New Deal understands the imperative to move away from oil, coal, and uranium as energy sources. Many investment firms are still making large investments in oil, coal, and uranium. This is a serious problem that needs to be brought to public attention because we need to make sure that capital is directed toward wind, solar, fuel cells, and other green energy technologies. We have to strengthen the connection between sustainability and profit, so that the most profitable industries of the future are those that are attuned to environmental consciousness. We need to begin a dialogue with Wall Street to ensure that we have a green investment strategy in the United States.

This is the time for our nation to tap the creative abilities of the National Aeronautics and Space Administration (NASA).

At Glenn Research Center in Cleveland, they have been doing research for many years on carbonless burns. We need to invest heavily in green energy research, so the government can develop [such energy] at the alpha stage, turn it over to the private sector at the beta stage, and create an economy that is based on profitability and sustainability, linked together. Sustainability ought to be very profitable, and when we make that link, we know that the green of the dollar bill will take on a new meaning.

We can also help jumpstart the green economy with a new program like the WPA (Works Progress Administration) of the 1930s. We could have a green energy program creating millions of jobs building green housing, retrofitting buildings with energy-saving technology, taking green microtechnologies, installing them domestically, building new jobs, spurring economic growth; we could call it the GWA, the Green Work Administration, creating millions of new jobs.

We have to understand the effects of global warming and global *warring*, because war is ecocide. War destroys the environment, so we must stand for peace. Peace and sustainability are intimately linked, and that linkage is our path to the future. A green peace symbol could unite us in defense of our right to survive.

The U.S. invasion of Iraq reveals the destructive connection between our nation's energy policy and our warped foreign policy. We need to say, "No more." We must end this effort to grab the oil of Iraq. We must not attack Iran. We must stop looking at oil as a resource to be seized by force.

Peace and sustainability are one, and we must confront the threat of nuclear weapons and understand that a nuclear strike anywhere would bring about a nuclear winter. We need to do everything we can to move toward the abolition of all nuclear weapons. This is what the nuclear nonproliferation treaty is about. We cannot talk about saving our planet if we ignore the fact that every one of those nuclear weapons is a threat to the survival of all species on the planet. We have a responsibility as people who believe in green consciousness to stand for peace and for nuclear abolition.

Peace and sustainability—that is the goal of the proposed cabinet-level Department of Peace and Nonviolence. We need to understand that when we come into harmony with nature, it is easier to come into harmony with each other. Domestic violence, spousal abuse, child abuse, violence in the schools, the campus violence, racial violence—all represent a disconnect from our own inner harmony, and it is the lack of connection with nature that causes a disconnect from our own inner harmony.

With the industrial revolution, we became so closely tied to our machines that we lost some of our humanity. We need to recapture our deeper sense of what it means to be human, and this is what environmental consciousness at the highest level is really about. It is about being fully human once again, being able to stand in a field during the summer and feel that warm breeze wash over you, and understand that that is a right that we have as human beings. We understand that is our right as human beings, being able to have the kind of attunement with nature that seems to have been lost and is somehow the province only of romantic poets. We need to recapture what it means to be close to nature. This is a spiritual quest.

It was in 1961 that President John F. Kennedy called for a united effort to reach the moon. President Kennedy proclaimed that our quest for moving into outer space was an example of how we could unite our country in a great cause. I believe that now is the time and that the American people are waiting for that kind of leadership, which brings us together in this common cause, which calls forward from each person in this country, this open heartedness to reach out to each other, to sustain each other, and to sustain our planet.

I think the American people are ready for such a call. I think the American people are ready to practice conservation in a very meaningful way. I think the American people are ready to make wiser choices in their products. I think the American people are ready to make wiser choices in their transportation. The American people are waiting to be united. We understand that human unity is the underpinning of our planet. We understand that the world needs to live as one. We understand the world is interconnected and interdependent; and because we understand that, we shall unite as a nation, we shall unite as a people, we shall put the cause of green energy, green environment, green peace, green action at the front of the American agenda, and we will do it out of love, and we will do it out of hope, and we will do it out of compassion, and we will do it by creating a new future.

Corporate Power Is
the Issue of the Day

RALPH NADER

*Ralph Nader became famous in 1965 when his indictment of
the American automobile industry,* Unsafe at Any Speed,
*was published. It led to such widely accepted regulations as fed-
eral performance standards for motor vehicles. Nader helped
pass at least eight major consumer protection laws, including
the Safe Drinking Water Act, and the founding of such regulatory agencies as the Occupational Safety and Health Administration, the Environmental Protection Agency, and the
Consumer Product Safety Administration. He has founded
many organizations, the largest of which is Public Citizen,
with a membership of over 100,000.*

A central political issue of our time is corporate power, and
the takeover of our government and the spread of commercial values into every nook and cranny of our culture:
the commercialization of childhood, the commercialization of
universities, and the commercialization of almost everything
these large companies touch.

We have to focus on the impacts of giant multinational corporations, which have subverted even capitalist principles by refusing to give their owners—the stockholders—any kind of authority. They also subvert a principle of capitalism, which if you cannot make it in the market, you go down; instead, they go to Washington for a bailout. The only true capitalists in this country are the small businesses. They are the only ones who are free to go bankrupt and aren't able to go to Washington for a bailout.

Giant corporations transcend national boundaries. They can circumvent the laws of nations, states, and localities. Like giants astride the globe, they are able to avoid accountability, avoid monitoring by elected officials, and avoid the courts as they pit one country against another.

There was a recent report saying tort lawyers are having trouble suing nursing home chains for mistreatment of elderly people. The reason is these nursing homes are owned by tiers of corporations. Some of them are offshore, and the most immediate tier has very few assets. So, they cannot be responsible for paying the verdicts, and more and more people are mistreated or neglected in those nursing homes with impunity.

In 2000, *Business Week*, the corporate magazine with the biggest circulation, had a cover story asking, "Too Much Corporate Power?" with six detailed pages saying, "yes, yes, yes." It polled the public, and 72 percent of the American people thought corporations have too much control over our lives.

You can imagine what that poll would register today, seeing as it registered 72 percent *before* Enron, WorldCom, Adelphia, HealthSouth, and all the other corporate criminals had been exposed. So we don't have an uphill battle with public opinion.

Yet every day, the imbalance of power between giant corporations and we the people gets worse. In Washington, D.C., when you ask any department of the U.S. government, "What is the most powerful external force on this agency?" the answer is the same: corporate power.

There are 35,000 full-time corporate lobbyists in Washington, D.C. There are 10,000 political action committees through which corporations funnel money to members of Congress and the White House. The drug industry alone has 500 full-time lobbyists on Capitol Hill; that is how they got the hundreds of billions of dollars from what is called the drug benefit bill, only it benefited the drug companies more than the patients or the taxpayers who are footing the bill.

When you hear people say, "The government isn't doing this or doing that," we should apply an adjective: it is the *corporate* government that isn't doing this or that. It is the *corporate* government that ignores the needs of tens of millions of impoverished people. Let's not use euphemisms such as *privatization*, when the more accurate term is *corporatization*. Let's not talk about the "private sector," when we know the phrase is the corporate sector.

When we talk about welfare, let's talk about the biggest amount of welfare money there ever was: corporate welfare. General Electric is on corporate welfare; Intel is on corporate welfare; Cisco is on corporate welfare; Microsoft is on corporate welfare; Pfizer is on corporate welfare; Merck is on corporate welfare. I challenge you to find one large company that is not on corporate welfare.

The nuclear industry wants to build more power plants. They can't meet the market test—they're not profitable—so they got the U.S. Senate to pass a $50 billion loan guarantee provision, mostly for new nuclear plants. And that is why corporate welfare is way larger than poor people welfare; because the large corporations are able to rent the loyalty of our lawmakers.

Throughout history there has been a struggle between commercial values and civic values. The values of profiteering, against the values of justice, tolerance, health, safety, regard for posterity, access to justice.

Every politician running for office, at whatever level, should be asked the cardinal question, "What have you done to shift power from the few who now control our country to the many who are supposed to control a true democracy?"

There are ways to give people more control of our democracy. We could expand the tort system so people who are injured by corporate misbehavior can take the perpetrators to court. Workplace safety is not an insignificant issue; 58,000 Americans die every year from work-related diseases and trauma. A hundred thousand Americans die every year from medical malpractice in hospitals alone; some 65,000 Americans die every year from air pollution.

Whoever controls the yardsticks by which a society is measured will control the agenda. We have to develop new yardsticks. When Alan Greenspan was chairman of the Federal Reserve, he would go up to Congress and talk about profits, gross national product, inventory levels, capital accumulation. What if there were other yardsticks he had to report on? What if he said, "Mr. Chairman, the state of our economy is not good for 80 percent of the American people; 80 million people live in poverty," contrary to the absurd definition of poverty by the Labor Department, which defines poverty as a family of four making under $19,000 a year. Thirteen million children go to bed hungry every night in the land of the free, home of the brave. Fifty million people make under $10.50 an hour, 45 to 48 million people do not have any health insurance, and 18,000 people in this country die every year because they cannot afford health insurance.

We must have our own people's economic yardsticks by which to measure our economy. We should not use corporate yardsticks to measure the economy. Whoever controls the yardsticks will control the way we look at the world. In analyzing whom we should pay attention to, it helps to ask one single question. If millions of people do not have health care, who is saying no to their getting health care? The HMOs, the drug companies, the hospital chains? If tens of millions of people don't have a living wage, who is saying no to a living wage? The Wal-Marts, the Kmarts, the McDonald's, the Burger Kings? If tens of millions of people are happy to pay more taxes than they should and the rich and powerful and corporate are paying far less than they should, who is saying no to progressive tax reform? It is these corporations and their executives. Who is saying no to cleaning up the election process? It is corporate money that is saying no.

Our economy now is about 20 to 25 times more productive per worker (adjusted for inflation) than it was in 1900. In 1900, there were poor people, there were hungry people, there were people without adequate shelter; and in 2007, there are poor people, there are hungry people, there are people without adequate shelter. They may have television sets now, where they did not in 1900, but how can an economy grow 20 to 25 times more productive per capita and still not have abolished poverty, still not have provided decent housing, still not have medical insurance for all?

It is because the corporate system is inherently defective; no matter how it grows, it will concentrate most of the wealth into the pockets of the top 5 percent of the population. The Fortune 500 CEOs are making between 400 to 500 times more than the average worker. The head of Wal-Mart made $11,000 per hour on average last year, and hundreds of thousands of his workers were making $7 to $10 an hour. And the gap keeps growing.

So, what do we do about all this? First, we have to split the corporate entity from the entity known as a human being. Corporations must be structurally, constitutionally, and operationally subordinated to the sovereignty of the people. They should be prohibited from contributing to elections and from participating in politics.

How did we ever get in this situation? A Supreme Court decision in 1886 decided that corporations were human beings for purposes of the Constitution; talk about right-wing judicial activism—it wasn't even argued by the lawyers in the Supreme Court. They just decreed it in the liner notes to the decision. The railroad company in this case was considered a person for purposes of the Fourteenth Amendment. What kind of society is it that gives an inanimate entity the same rights that we humans have? Corporations don't vote, they don't die in Iraq, they don't have children, so they should not have these constitutional rights.

I am pleased to say that all over the country people are raising the issue of corporate personhood, due mostly to the work of the Program on Corporations, Law and Democracy (POCLAD), founded by Richard Grossman and others more than 15 years ago. Corporations should not be treated as persons. Personhood should be taken away from these corporate entities.

We have to redefine the agreement between the society and the giant corporate entity. The best way to do that is to abolish state chartering of corporations. We need to set up the federal chartering of large corporations. In the early days, around 1800, when the first corporations were chartered in the state of Massachusetts to manufacture textiles, the legislature chartered one at a time. They put them on a short leash. The charters had an expiration date and had to be renewed. Back then corporations were seen as our servants, not our masters. Once we raise the issue of federal charters, all kinds of issues of corporate accountability, of corporate compliance, of disempowering corporations, of giving more power to the consumers and workers and pension funds, come to the forefront. It is a framework for shifting power back to the sovereignty of the people away from the giant corporations. What is the word here? The word is *subordination*. I urge you to use that word. We must create a movement for subordinating corporate power to the supremacy of the citizens.

The second approach is displacement of corporate products, services, and that is what the Green Festivals are about, displacement. It is saying, "We are going to replace corporate agribusiness and genetically modified food with the preservation of the small farm, and organic agriculture, and farmers' markets." Displacement means full Medicare for all, which displaces just the way Medicare for the elderly did in the 1960s—it displaces the health insurance industry.

Solar energy—decentralized, distributed through co-ops and other nongiant corporate delivery systems—displaces more and more of the fossil fuel giants Exxon and Peabody Coal. That is displacement. By refusing to enter McDonald's, refusing to enter Starbucks, refusing to enter Wal-Marts, you are strengthening the displacement movement.

We shouldn't let them pull down our standards or let them subordinate environment, labor, and consumer rights to the supremacy of corporate international trade. They are circumventing our democratic processes, our courts, our regulatory agencies, our legislature. You cannot buy anything in your hometown from child labor, products made from child labor in this country, because it is illegal. But because our country has signed onto the World Trade Organization (WTO), we cannot pass a law prohibiting the importation of products made by child labor abroad because that would violate the WTO, and a country that would take us to Geneva would beat us in those secret courts under the WTO. We couldn't have been first with airbags if the WTO had been around then. We would have had to go to "harmonization committees" organized by WTO bureaucrats in Switzerland, where our standards would be driven downward by other countries on the committee who didn't want airbags to be mandatory in cars.

Subordination and displacement: Why do I emphasize these kinds of approaches? Because giant corporations have learned to game our system. They have learned to neutralize regulatory agencies. They have learned to buy elections. They have learned to block access to the courts. They have learned to get into the minds of our young children, so that their very trademarks with this mass marketing undermining parental authority, selling pornography, violence, junk food, junk drink, dangerous toys. They are getting into the minds of our children at a very young age. They have learned how to engage in greenwashing. They have learned how to co-opt many good environmental groups.

That means we must confront them with a new strategy. First, we take away their symbols: the American flag is ours; the Pledge of Allegiance is ours. The Pledge of Allegiance ends with a phrase the corporations cannot pledge allegiance to; it ends with the phrase "with liberty and justice for all."

What is the single-most important institution that can turn it around? Congress has enormous constitutional authority, far greater than the executive and the judiciary, which is why it is surrendering so much of it on the installment plan to both the executive and the judiciary. About 1,500 corporations with

offices in Washington pretty much get their way with a majority of 535 members of Congress, but we are millions of people.
The corporations have a lot of money, but they don't have a single vote. We are 600,000 people in each congressional district
on average. If we were to put the energy into organizing Congress watchdog organizations in every congregational district,
with at least the level of energy that is exhibited by a serious
bird-watching club or bowling league, you would see a dramatic
difference in the behavior of your senators and representatives.

The critical mass is about 2,000 people per district, who
choose watching Congress as their principal hobby, who learn
the skills of holding Congress accountable, who learn the talents of getting their member of Congress into local auditoriums
where they are grilled before a local media and full assemblage;
2,000 people per congressional district focusing on just a half
dozen issues, health care being one, and subordination of corporations being two, for starters. If we don't create that level of
monitoring, we are not going to challenge corporate power.

We must get people to give a damn about how this country
is run. Even though the citizens get ripped off, disrespected,
excluded, when you ask them, "Do they know the name of the
person representing you in Congress?" they usually can't tell you
that simple fact.

The greatest obstacle to the rise of a functioning, sustainable democracy is the belief by millions of people that they are
powerless. They don't count and they don't matter. That's the
way we grow up as children. As my father said to me when I was
10 years old and I came home from school, "Ralph, what did
you learn in school today? Did you learn how to believe, or did
you learn how to think?" I thought about that one for a long
time. That is why we have to pay attention to the introduction

of civic skills in our elementary and high schools. Not civics, civic skills—connecting the classroom to the community. No one can stop us from doing that. We are parents, citizens, taxpayers, and we can get it done. The children love it when they are given the opportunity to learn by getting out in the community with meaningful projects.

Let us total up our assets. I have described the assets of power of corporations. A lot of their assets actually belong to us. The timber companies, oil and gas companies, uranium companies, gold companies—they are getting minerals from public lands, either free or for bargain basement prices. The public lands belong to us, but we have allowed corporations to control what we own, to profit from what we own, to exploit what we own, to pollute from what we own.

The public airways belong to us. That is a tremendous asset, but the Federal Communications Commission (FCC) gives it away, and the media corporations don't pay anything to us, the landlords. The radio and TV stations are the tenants, and they get away, since 1927, with not a paying rent for the most powerful property in the country: the public airwaves. If we were to charge them rent, it would be a lot of money. And with that money we could have airtime every day, and we could build our own TV and radio studios, and hire our own reporters and producers. Just imagine what we could do.

Those are some of our assets, but no asset is greater than an aroused mind in an aroused citizen who is communicating with other people. Word of mouth is the fastest, most credible form of communication, with friends, relatives, coworkers, people you meet in the supermarket line. If people spent as much time talking about impeaching Dick Cheney and George W. Bush as they do talking about *American Idol*, we would have it done.

If there is one cardinal lesson of history, it is that the people only get what they demand and fight for. As the great abolitionist Frederick Douglas said, "Power concedes nothing without a demand." You couple that with Cicero's definition, "Freedom is participation in power," and tie it to the saying ascribed to the fifteenth-century Chinese general Wang Yang Ming, "To know, and not to act, is not to know."

The time to act is now. We *can* change the course of history if we believe in our collective power and dedicate enough, time, energy and talent toward a just society.

On Becoming
an Ecopreneur

BEN COHEN

Ben Cohen is a cofounder, along with Jerry Greenfield, of Ben & Jerry's ice cream company. He is also the cofounder of two nonprofit educational organizations, TrueMajority and Business Leaders for Sensible Priorities.

Jerry Greenfield and I were the slowest, fattest kids in the seventh grade gym class. The whole class was running around the track, and half a lap behind would be Jerry and me. After high school I didn't want to go to college. My father and sister filled out my college applications. I went to Colgate, dropped out, went to Skidmore, dropped out, went to New York University, dropped out, and dropped out of the New School in New York. I got into the most unstructured college program at the time, the University without Walls. I dropped out. Jerry went through four years of college, took pre-med, and was rejected from all 30 medical schools where he applied.

We figured if we were going to get anywhere, we were going to have to start our own business. The only thing we liked doing was eating, so it had to be a food business. We wanted to take a food trend in the big cities to a rural college town. Homemade ice cream was it. We stumbled upon this correspondence course in ice cream. It was a $5 course. We split one between us. We opened the business in May 1978 on an investment of $8,000.

In an effort to keep the business alive in winter, we packed our ice cream in pint containers to see if we could sell it that way. And that's really what made the business take off. After a few years Jerry and I looked at ourselves and said, "We're not spending our time making ice cream and scooping ice cream. We're hiring and firing, dealing with lawyers and accountants and correspondence, and trying to do the books."

This was not our idea of a good time. We decided to sell the business. I ran into an eccentric restaurateur I knew and told him we were selling. He said, "Ben, how could you do that? The business is your baby. It's just starting off. It has so much potential." And we said, "Maurice, business exploits the community, the environment, its workers." He said, "If you don't like the way business works, why don't you just change it?" That hadn't occurred to us.

We decided to keep the business and see if we could use it as a force for progressive social change. We decided to engage in an experiment to see if it was possible to use the tools of business to repair society.

We were in a 3,000-square-foot facility and bursting at the seams. We didn't have enough room for our raw ingredients or our finished product. Working conditions were poor; our ice cream equipment was old. We weren't able to make enough to fill our orders. We needed money to build a real ice cream plant.

The usual method for this is taking in venture capital: essentially lots of money from a few well-to-do people. We said,

"How could we use this need for cash so that as the business prospers, the community automatically prospers?" We wanted to sell stocks to Vermonters: people who had supported us from the beginning. The lawyers and accountants said, "There aren't that many people in Vermont. They don't have any money. And besides, the money is right there from these venture capitalists."

We held the first-ever in-state Vermont stock offering. We deliberately had a very low minimum buy of $126 to participate in this IPO, an opportunity that's usually only available to fairly sophisticated investors that have at least $2,000 to invest. We advertised the stock in the main section of the newspaper beside clothing and supermarket ads. It said, "Get a scoop of the action." We raised $750,000. One out of every 100 families became a shareholder in Ben & Jerry's.

We built the new plant, and entered our first major market, Boston. The ice cream was selling really well. Then Pillsbury bought Häagen-Dazs. We were distributing our ice cream through a network of independent ice cream distributors, who bought 20 to 30 different brands from different manufacturers and then distributed them to stores. The Pillsbury salespeople told our distributor, "If you continue to sell Ben & Jerry's, we're not going to sell you Häagen-Dazs anymore." Häagen-Dazs was the established brand. Distributors couldn't afford to be without it. Their customers demanded it. They were going to drop our product. If that happened, it would be the end of our business because the same thing would happen all over the country.

A lawyer told us that was a restraint of trade under federal antitrust law that says that the company that controls the major share of a given market can't use its power and economic strength to keep others out of the market. But the lawyer also said that the Federal Trade Commission wasn't really in the business of protecting small businesses; it was protecting large businesses. We realized that we weren't going to get very far in a lawsuit against a $4 billion corporation with a large team of lawyers.

So we started the "What's the Doughboy afraid of?" campaign. We held a press conference. Two reporters showed up. Jerry was a one-man picketer outside the Pillsbury headquarters in Minneapolis.

We thought, "Well, who really cares if Ben & Jerry's goes down the tubes? The people who buy the ice cream." So we put this sticker on the side of our containers that said, "What's the Doughboy afraid of?" with an 800 number. People would call and get a recording from us with our story and asking people to leave their name and address for their Doughboy Kit. That kit included a write-in letter to the Federal Trade Commission, a write-in letter to the chairman of the board of Pillsbury, a pamphlet talking about what was going on, a "What's the Doughboy afraid of?" bumper sticker, and a chance to send in $10 and get a T-shirt. We got about 100 calls a day.

Eventually, the news media noticed—a big article in the *New Yorker* magazine, the cover of the Sunday magazine of the *Boston Globe*, the *Hartford Courant*, and the *Wall Street Journal*. Pillsbury finally relented.

Years later we needed more money, so we held a national public stock offering. We also wanted to be of service to the community, to give away as much money as possible, so we created the Ben & Jerry's Foundation, which told people who bought the stock that 7.5 percent of our pretax profit was being donated. That was the highest amount of any publicly held company. That foundation lasted a year. It was totally overrun by grant requests from incredibly worthwhile organizations dealing with issues of poverty, education, housing, hunger, and domestic abuse. We could only fund about 5 percent of them.

We realized that just giving away money wasn't going to solve the problem.

We said, "Business is a combination of organized human energy plus money, which equals power." Business has now become the most powerful force in the world. But that's a new phenomenon that has only really occurred in my lifetime.

Business controls our media through ownership, our legislation through lobbyists, our elections through campaign contributions, and the lives of average citizens as employees and customers. All of this is done in the narrow self-interest of business without a concern for the common good. Religion and government had as their purpose improving the quality of life for everybody, but business has never had that as part of its mission. That's why today this most powerful force is hell-bent on maximizing short-term profits, and most companies are not worried about the fallout from this headlong rush toward short-term profitability.

Years ago Jerry and I went to a workshop with CEOs in Atlanta. They had CEOs from some of the largest companies in the country: the head of UPS, the head of The Home Depot. We discovered that they were good people who cared about the unmet needs of the society, gave of their own personal money and time to try to deal with these issues. We left the conference and thought, "Well, if business is the most powerful force in the society, and these huge corporations are being run by these CEOs who have these concerns, how come business isn't using its power to address those social issues?"

The answer has two parts. First, you only get what you measure. When you're on a diet, you regularly weigh yourself. Constantly measuring yourself keeps you aligned toward your goal and motivated to accomplish your objective. In business, the only way that we've measured success is by profit, and we've been motivated to seek that goal exclusively.

Also, we compartmentalize our lives. We deal with our social concerns by giving money or time; we deal with our spiritual concerns in church or temple or mosque; we deal with our financial needs in business. We must integrate those needs and concerns into our business world.

There is a spiritual aspect to business just as there is to individuals. As you give, you receive; as you help, you're helped. As your business supports the community, the community supports your business. Just because this idea is written in the Bible and not in some business textbook doesn't make it less valid. It's a major switch from a win-lose scenario to win-win. A switch from business versus the community, its employees, its customers, to business working together with them for the benefit of all. Despite this, it meets with incredible resistance in business schools.

We said, "If the problem is in how we measure success, why don't we just change the way we measure our success?" We redefined the bottom line. We called all our employees together and said, "From now on, the bottom line at Ben & Jerry's has two parts: How much have we improved the quality of life in the community? And how much profit is left over at the end of each month? If we haven't contributed to both those objectives, we have failed." Everybody stood up and applauded.

Our managers said, "You know, that sounded really good, but we discovered that when we put company time and energy and resources into improving the quality of life in the community, it takes away from the time and energy and resources that we can put into increasing profits and vice versa."

Most people say, "It's not possible for a business to be profitable and to work to meet social needs at the same time." We've all been brought up to believe that we deal with our social concerns in the nonprofit world and our financial concerns in the for-profit world. But once you change that mind-set, the opportunities to combine both are limitless.

This is not philanthropy; it's factoring in a third variable into the equation. Usually a business makes decisions based on price and quality or speed. We added in a third factor: the impact on the community. It makes it more interesting and more complex. Here are a few examples of how we did it at Ben & Jerry's.

I ran into Bernie Glassman, who was running a bakery whose purpose was to provide job training for formerly unemployable people—ex-convicts, the homeless, addicts—to help them get back into the workforce. We said, "If we can find some product that this bakery can make for us that we can use in our ice cream, we'll be able to sell that ice cream and make money, and also help that social enterprise." That's how the flavor Chocolate Fudge Brownie happened. Today we buy over $2 million a year worth of brownies from the Greyston Bakery.

We were making ice cream in Vermont, where one of the major socioeconomic problems was that the economy of many towns was based on family dairy farms, which were rapidly going out of business. We decided that all our milk and cream would come from Vermont family farms. When the artificial growth hormone rBGH came out, we decided that all our milk would not use rBGH.

We learned that the rainforest was being destroyed, and a study said that if the fruits and nuts growing there were harvested, the rainforests could be both sustained and as economically viable as when they were destroyed and turned into cattle ranches. That's how we came up with the flavor Rainforest Crunch, which was designed to maximize the use of Brazil nuts. Every Brazil nut ever eaten has been grown in the wild and sustainably harvested in the rainforest.

We developed a banking relationship with the Shore Bank, the first community development bank in the country. The paper we packed in was bleached in chlorine, so we ended up having the first ice cream container that used unbleached paper.

Eventually we wrote a book called *Ben & Jerry's Double-Dip: How to Lead with Your Values and Make Money, Too*. The idea was that perhaps the most powerful tool that business has is its voice. When business talks, politicians, the media, and the public listen.

Just over 10 years ago, a small group of businesspeople met to see if we could use business tools to understand why there are so many unmet needs in this richest country and what we could do about it. We became Business Leaders for Sensible Priorities, a nonprofit, nonpartisan organization with over 700 members, including the former heads of Hasbro, Phillips, Van Heusen, Visa, Goldman Sachs, and many unknowns.

First we looked at the federal budget. Housing, education, the environment, and community development get all these little slivers. The Pentagon grew to 50 percent of that pie chart during the Cold War, when we were in an arms race with the Soviet Union. So, we said, "Wouldn't it be possible to reduce that?"

We brought in a board of military advisers. They said that we currently spend tens of billions of dollars every year building obsolete weapons designed during the Cold War era. They were designed to fight a mass army of an enemy that no longer exists.

We need to cut money for weapons designed to fight the former Soviet Union. We currently have the most advanced fighter jets in the world. Nobody comes close. We are preparing to retire those jets early and replace them with a new generation of fighter jets that cost five times as much. We planned that when we thought the Soviet Union was going to build some. They went out of business, but we're going ahead with it anyhow.

We said, "Why don't we poll how the public feels about it?" And we found that once the public was aware of this, they wanted to shift twice that amount into social needs and out of the Pentagon. We introduced the Common Sense Budget Act, a piece of legislation that has been introduced to Congress, which redirects $60 billion.

In the Priorities Campaign and in this Common Sense Budget Act, we recommend taking $10 billion a year from the Pentagon and putting it into education. Over 12 years, that would be enough to repair every U.S. school that needs it. Take $15 billion and put it into world hunger: that's enough to provide food self-sufficiency for all of the 6 million kids a year that die of hunger around the world. Take $10 billion a year and put it into children's health care: that's enough money to provide health care to every kid in the United States who currently doesn't have health insurance. Take $10 billion a year over 10 years and put it into energy independence: that's enough money to reduce our need for oil by 50 percent through home insulation and economic incentives to manufacture hybrid cars.

We spend about $20 billion per year on our nuclear arsenal. We now have the equivalent of 100,000 Hiroshima-size bombs. At the Priorities Campaign our military advisers say that we can cut that amount in half, save $10 billion a year, and still have more than enough nuclear weapons to protect the vital self-interest of the United States.

Our country faces a huge challenge. As the last remaining superpower, we need to learn to measure strength not in terms of how many we can kill but in terms of how many we can feed, clothe, house, and care for. Making that change in priorities would make us a great nation again and restore the trust that was once placed in us by people all over the world.

PART THREE

Birthing the Green Economy

Making the Green Economy Work for Everyone

VAN JONES

Van Jones is the founder and president of the Ella Baker Center for Human Rights in Oakland, California. He recently started the group Green for All (greenforall.org), which is focused on bringing green-collar jobs into lower-income communities.

Many people have been working, hoping, and praying for years that some day the United States would wake up to the peril that we're facing and begin to respond. So to all of you who paved the way, for all of you who held that light of hope alive, I want to thank you and let you know that our time has finally come.

We are finally turning the corner in the direction of sanity. This will mean a different kind of challenge for us. It's one thing when your movement is small and on the fringe of society. But it's something else when your movement becomes the dominant movement, the main movement, the biggest movement in the country. And that's what this green movement is becoming.

This green economy movement is going to reverse the direction away from the suicidal capitalism that has been destroying our environment, toward something green and beautiful. But as this movement moves from the margin to the center, there is a key question we must address: who are we going to take with us, and who are we going to leave behind?

We have a moral and political obligation to say that we're not just building a green economy for the people who can afford to buy a Prius or put a set of solar panels on their second home. We are building a green economy strong enough to lift people out of poverty, and we want to be judged based on that.

Coming out of urban America, I've been to more funerals than Green Festivals. We have communities in Oakland, Watts, the South Bronx, and Newark that need new opportunities to build wealth and to improve our health. When I think about the green economy that is being created, my spirits are lifted, because I know some new jobs are coming. And so are new technologies, products, services, opportunities to build wealth, and if we stand together and expand the coalition to include more people, we can save the polar bears, and we can save the black kids, too.

When I first got started in this, I was not an environmentalist. I have been working to get youth who were in prison out of prison, and I came across a contradiction. Our society says to inner-city youth that if they are engaged in economic activities that are hurting people, selling drugs, stealing cars, we say, "You go to jail." But when those young people get out of jail and come home, if we give them a job in a factory where we're polluting the planet, making products that poison everybody, we call it a success story. How is it rational that I'm fighting to get young people out of jail so they can get jobs that detract from the health of my community?

We must have a new standard for these young people. We should get them engaged in beautiful, dignified, uplifting, powerful, hopeful, helpful work, and we cannot accept anything less than that for all our children.

We are now entering what I call the third wave of environmentalism. The first wave was a conservation wave. Some people think about Teddy Roosevelt, but the original conservationists were the Native Americans. They were so good at what they did, that you had in North America a fully populated continent. When we talk about conservation, let's make sure we always honor the original conservationists, the Native Americans. Then, in 1492, the continent was put under new management. After 400 years of extreme resource exploitation, you had to have a conservation movement of people saying, "Hold on, we can't cut down *every* tree. We can't pave the *whole* continent." And those people were the conservationists that we celebrate. And their beautiful legacy continues to this day.

Then came the second wave: the regulation wave. In 1963, Rachel Carson wrote the book *Silent Spring*,[1] and it changed the conversation on a huge scale. She established the fact that environmentalism is not just about plants, critters, and babbling brooks. As important as those are, conservation is also about human beings, human health effects, and how we are poisoning our own bodies and our children with our industrial lifestyle. That message laid the foundation for the Clean Air Act, the Clean Water Act, the Environmental Protection Agency, and Earth Day. It was a beautiful moment in American democracy.

Yet there was a problem with the regulation wave: There was too little attention paid to race, class, income, and power. To some people of color and poor folks it almost looked like the white mainstream environmental movement was conspiring with the big white polluters, when we saw toxic waste dumps being concentrated in black, brown, and poor communities, and the data mounted showing diseases such as asthma and cancer multiplying among the poor.

In response, in the 1980s, a new movement emerged called the environmental justice movement. This movement said, "Our children shouldn't have to be poisoned or walk around with asthma inhalers or bear the brunt of the toxic burden of society. Regulate it, yes, but regulate it fairly. Don't regulate it onto poor children."

Now the third wave is taking off, and it is fundamentally different. The first wave was about conserving the beauty and the bounty of the past. The second wave was about regulating the problems of the industrial present. This new wave is about investing in the solutions of the future. This new wave is not just about regulating the bad stuff; it's about investing in the good stuff—renewable energy, organic agriculture, hybrid engines, high-performance buildings, biofuels, and all the clean and green new technologies—the solutions we need.

But what is the meaning for people of color in this new wave? Is there an opportunity for us to be a part of this, or are we going to repeat the mistakes we made in the second wave?

When I raise this issue to people of color, some say, "Well, I don't even want to be in the green wave. The green wave is just a bunch of hippies." Then I have to show them how big this movement has become and what a huge part of the economy it is, and that's why I'm desperate to make sure this is an inclusive movement.

Green has now gone mainstream. On a cultural level, it's Cameron Diaz getting into her hybrid; it's George Clooney with his electric car. *Vanity Fair* has had big green issues. *Elle* magazine came out with a green issue, saying, "Green is the new black." Al Gore got an Oscar, and any time a politician gets an Oscar for doing something, you know it's a big deal. So just on a pop cultural level, you know something major is happening. Celebrities promoting green values are a very good thing.

There has been a massive increase in what we call greenwashing—this ridiculous process where big polluters are running ads portraying themselves as green: General Electric with Ecomagination, Honda with Environment-ology, and Lexus saying, "Corners and trees both deserve to be hugged." Now this is farcical, but why are they doing it? They're doing it because they know that there are millions of people out there who want to buy green products, and the companies are trying to get in on that market.

So how big is this market? The sector of the economy known as LOHAS (Lifestyles of Health and Sustainability) is already a multibillion-dollar part of the economy. That's the good news.

The bad news is that this is probably the most racially segregated part of the U.S. economy, by owners, workers, consumers, any way you want to look at it. So, we need to ask, How do we open up this sector to include as many people as possible, so this green wave can lift all boats?

I see three possible futures. One is what I call *ecoapocalypse*: we just keep doing what we're doing; we keep killing living things; we keep turning nature into commodities; and we destroy the biological basis of human existence, resulting in a massive die-off of our species.

The second scenario is also terrifying: I call it *ecoapartheid*. One mother is on a yoga mat while her nanny is taking her child to school in the Prius, and the other mother is working two low-wage jobs and has a child with asthma from living near a factory spewing toxins into the air. Ecoapartheid is not only immoral, it will not work. It will breed resentment and lead to violent rebellion. Ecoapartheid is just a speed bump on the road to ecoapocalypse.

The only solution is what I call *ecoequity*. It's about equal access and equal opportunity to the best of the green economy. We should merge our civil rights agenda and our environmental agenda by building a green economy strong and inclusive enough to lift people out of poverty. It's not about "You're wrong and I'm right." It's about "Our children won't have a planet to live on if we don't get together and figure this thing out so everyone is included."

Polar Bears and Poor Kids

When the affluent think about the environmental crisis, they say, "Oh, my God, the polar bears are drowning because of global warming." Are they right or wrong to focus on that? They're right. Why? Because the polar bears have an inherent right to live, just like we do. So somebody needs to defend them.

But if I go to West Oakland or Watts or the South Bronx and knock on doors, and try to tell people about the polar bears, they're not feeling me at all. When poor people think about environmental problems, they think about asthma, cancer, gas prices, the things that hit at the poverty level. They are more likely to be concerned about people drowning in New Orleans during Hurricane Katrina because of government inaction than polar bears drowning because of global warming.

When rich people think about environmental solutions, what do they think about? Hybrid cars and solar panels, right? They think of recycling, solar power, and all the new organic products. They think about business opportunities and consumer choices. Are they right or wrong to focus on that? They're right. We want rich people to invest in products that help the Earth rather than hurt the Earth. We want consumers with disposable income to spend it in ways that help the Earth rather than hurt the Earth.

But the question we have to ask is, What is the meaning of the green economy for the poor majority of this planet? And the best answer is green-collar jobs, green entrepreneurial opportunities, and green community investments. The green economy can no longer be just a place for affluent people to spend money; it must also be a place for ordinary people to earn money.

At the Ella Baker Center, we have been working hard to get good green jobs for the young brothers and sisters who have been locked out of the old pollution-based economy. If you teach a young person how to put up solar panels, she is on her way to becoming an electrical engineer. It is a green pathway out of poverty. If you train a young person to install energy-efficient windows, he is on his way to becoming a glazer. That's a well-paid union job.

We learned that most carpenters don't know how to work with anything but wood, a depleting resource. We learned that if you can work with bamboo—which is a grass that grows very rapidly—you are helping the Earth by using a product that is more renewable than wood, and you are developing skills that are increasingly in demand and pay good wages. You're helping nature, but it's also the first step on the ladder toward a career, toward entrepreneurship, toward ownership, toward empowerment.

So we want to create a green jobs corps in Oakland, California. We went to our community colleges, our city council, and our community leaders, and we asked them, "Will you work with us?" There's a labor shortage right now in these specialized jobs. Can we build a green pathway out of poverty for our young people in Oakland? And they said, "Yes."

We didn't know that some people had noticed what we were doing. And we got a phone call from somebody, and the name was scribbled down wrong, and I didn't even know who it was, and we almost missed the meeting, and I finally asked somebody to call them back and said, "Who's calling us?" And the phone call was from Nancy Pelosi, the Speaker of the House, who was in San Francisco, and she said, "Come on over and talk to us, and tell us what you're doing." And as a result of that, we sat down with her, and we told her what our dream was, and we told her what we were hoping for. And we told her, "You are the most powerful woman ever in the history of U.S. politics. You're the third-most powerful person in the country. If Bush and Cheney choke on a pretzel, you're the president."

We told her that we've got a generation of children, our youth, who nobody has ever reached out to and told them anything but "Don't shoot somebody; don't get pregnant; don't do drugs." But nobody stood up for them and said, "I love you, and I believe in you, and I want you to be a part of something. I want you to stand with me to retrofit this whole country. I want you to stand with me to reenergize America. I want you to stand with me and be at the center of this movement." We said to Nancy Pelosi, "If you do that, you will change America."

And the Speaker agreed with us, and we worked with her to insert a green jobs provision in the energy bill that passed both houses of Congress and President Bush signed into law in December 2007.

We're beginning to build this green pathway out of poverty. So now it's your turn. Those of you who are consumers, investors, policymakers, now it's your turn. We need you to stand with us. We need you to go to your own local colleges and say, "Give us some of these young people. We want to reach out and include more people, and give more people an opportunity."

This is a tremendous opportunity. For the first time since Bobby Kennedy and Martin Luther King Jr. were killed in 1968, we can build a movement that crosses the lines of race and class, and transforms this economy from the bottom up. We need to move forward together, hand in hand, to build one of those great coalitions, like the New Deal Coalition, that redefines what government is all about. We need to get the government on the side of the problem solvers in the economy and not the problem makers.

We'll be saying, "We want America to lead the world, but not in war, not in pollution, not in incarceration rates. We want America to lead the world in clean and green solutions. We want America to lead the world in bringing a multiracial country together, solving tough problems. And we want America to lead the world in something beautiful." When we do that, we won't be taking America back; we'll be taking America forward.

Note

1. Rachel Carson also wrote three other books: *Under the Sea-Wind* (New York: Oxford University Press, 1941); *The Sea around Us* (New York: Oxford University Press, 1951); *The Edge of the Sea* (Boston: Houghton Mifflin, 1955).

Green Careers:
The New Frontier

MARIE KERPAN

Marie Kerpan is the founder of Green Careers, a career consulting practice. She teaches in the Green MBA Program at Dominican University in San Rafael, California. Marie is the author of "Balance: The Ultimate Challenge of the 21st Century," published in an anthology of essays entitled When the Canary Stops Singing: Women's Perspectives on Transforming Business.

M y purpose here is to inspire you to take steps toward having a green career. We've got a lot of work to do, and everyone's skills and experience are needed.

Green careers are the solution to the ecological, social, and economic problems of our time. I see green careers as the antidote to the depression, anxiety, and powerlessness that we often feel in the face of the huge challenges we're facing as a global community.

What can we do about global warming, climate change, pollution, ecological sustainability, and social injustice? The main thing we can do is to use our skills, experience, and creativity to work on whatever problems interest us the most. Aligning your interests, skills, and values with your work is one of the most powerful things you can do to make a difference in the world and in your life.

There has been a paradigm shift in the way we think about green careers. While traditional green careers like natural resource conservation and protection, and pollution control and remediation continue to be important, we now realize that we need to redesign everything from the ground up to be sustainable. We need to prevent pollution, eliminate waste, and rethink the way we do everything from a systems perspective. We have to take into account the impacts of our actions on our environment, be it human or otherwise. We can't just take the money and run.

If we want to sell or buy chocolate, we need to care whether the cocoa beans were organically grown, whether the people who grew them were paid a fair wage, and whether the beans really need to be transported to Switzerland to be processed before being shipped all over the world. We need to ask, Is this a sustainable enterprise? If not, how can we creatively make it so?

We cannot continue to see the world in a compartmentalized way. We need to redesign how we live, produce, consume, and waste from a holistic perspective. And there's urgency because we're running out of natural resources and climate change is upon us. We need to change the way we live because there aren't enough natural resources on the planet to accommodate us at our current levels of consumption. If everyone on Earth lived the way we do in America, we would need three to four planet Earths to provide the necessary natural resources. A typical European footprint (a measure of resource consumption) is half the size of a typical American footprint, so we have something to learn about living sustainably from our neighbors across the Atlantic.

It's time to ask tough questions about our work. Is it useful? Is it satisfying? Does it solve an authentic need? Is it contributing to the problems we're facing? Are we really bringing our talents and gifts to bear on solving problems or creating meaningful solutions?

Here's the good news. There's great personal satisfaction in doing meaningful work to solve our ecological problems. Everyone's skills, talents, and experience are needed. And there's plenty of money to be made. I keep hearing the media perpetuate the myth that a green career means you're going to have to take a cut in pay. I don't subscribe to that at all. This is a new frontier, and there are fortunes being made as we speak, and there is money in it for everybody.

Let's look at the career growth areas of the emerging green economy. There are four front-runners:

- Energy conservation and conversion to renewable sources of energy,
- Green building,
- Alternative transportation and biofuels,
- Sustainable agriculture.

These sectors are in the forefront of the emerging green economy because they most directly address our biggest challenge: global warming and the resulting climate change.

How are these four career tracks related to global warming, and what are the career implications? We know that we must reduce our greenhouse gas emissions in order to mitigate the impact of climate change. The quickest and best way to do that is by reducing our energy consumption and switching to renewable sources of energy like solar, wind, and biomass. By doing so, we reduce our greenhouse gas emissions and reduce our dependence on fossil fuels. This challenge presents exciting career opportunities in improving energy conservation and in the sourcing and application of various types of renewable energy. Careers promoting change in energy policy and practices through education and advocacy in nonprofit organizations or by working on public policy at various levels of government are critical to moving the agenda forward. Strategies and solutions are being developed through technology, business, policy, politics, and public education using all types of media.

For an overview of the wide range of new career possibilities in the clean technology arena, I recommend *The Clean Tech Revolution* by Ron Pernick and Clint Wilder. It includes names of organizations that could be potential employers or investment opportunities.

There are two main sectors that present the biggest opportunity for conservation of energy and for conversion to renewable sources of energy—namely, building design and construction, and transportation. This opens up careers in what we now call green building, where we aim to design buildings that are more energy-efficient and less dependent on fossil fuels. Green buildings also conserve water and natural resources and use renewable, nontoxic materials, among other sustainability goals. Careers in green building cover many disciplines, from architecture, landscaping, engineering, and construction, to the development of building materials that are nontoxic and recyclable.

Transportation is the other sector where we can achieve major gains in energy conservation and conversion to renewables in the area of biofuels, energy-efficient vehicles, public transit, ferries, light rail, bicycles, and scooters. Here again a multidisciplinary approach is needed including technical expertise as well as public education, political pressure, policy analyses and development, and business savvy.

The final career track is sustainable agriculture, by which we mean the shift from industrial agriculture to local, organic food production. How is this related to climate change? Industrial agriculture is very dependent on fossil fuels to run farm equipment, produce fertilizer, and pesticides and to transport food long distances. Local organic farms use less fossil fuel because they use natural fertilizers and pesticides and they don't transport their products long distances. Organic farming is also more sustainable because it eliminates the toxic chemicals, fertilizers, and pesticides that pollute the land, air, and food, causing illness in animals and humans, not to mention the workers who are working in the fields. The work that needs to be done in this fast-growing sector is to connect communities to their local organic sources of food and support the growth of local farmers. In Marin County, organic farms are connected with local schools, restaurants, and grocers. We need to find creative ways to make organic food available to everyone, educate the public about the benefits of eating local organic food, and build demand in the marketplace, working to make sure that organic standards aren't compromised. All of this work requires a team approach involving many different kinds of careers.

Green careers take many forms. They can be technical or nontechnical, for profit or not for profit. Green jobs can be found in large corporations, small businesses, or the public sector at the federal, state, or local levels of government.

There is a tendency to think that you need a technical background of some kind to find a green job, but every organization needs people to do the classic functions of general management, operations, marketing, sales, fund-raising, administration, accounting and financial management, strategic planning, human resources, customer service, and on and on. Every job title that you see in any corporate setting can be a green job if you are working in the context of sustainability solutions.

These four career tracks, while they are at the forefront of the green economy, are really the tip of the iceberg, as you can see by going to one of the Green Festivals (greenfestivals.org). There are so many different kinds of businesses that are working on different aspects of sustainability.

We are challenged with redesigning everything—our products, our processes, our services, and our communities—to be more aligned with sustaining life on our planet. Water conservation and purification is a huge one. Addressing population growth and land use, restoring natural habitat to reverse species extinction, preventing pollution in all of its forms, improving ecological literacy, building sustainable communities and local economies—these are the challenges of our time. This is a new frontier, and everyone's skill and experience are relevant and needed.

How do you find your place in all of this? The big question people come to me with is, How do I translate my skills, interest, and experience into a green career? There are two things you need to do. One is to identify what your interests are in the green space, which is why events like the Green Festivals are so valuable because they provide a place for the team to come together and show off what everyone is doing. Ultimately, you need to focus your search on the area that interests you the most.

The second thing you need to do is identify your motivated skills. And by that I mean, what are the skills that you enjoy using? We all have lots of skills, and often the skills you're using at work are not the ones you enjoy using the most. There's no need to continue to do something you don't enjoy. The object is to provide a useful product or service and enjoy it! Work should be an expression of your natural talent, values, and interests. When your skills, values, and interests are aligned, you're most likely to be successful and satisfied with your career.

Don't worry so much about "where the action is" or trying to find the hot careers. Instead, ask yourself, What do I really want to contribute? What do I bring to the party that nobody else has? Everybody has a unique constellation of gifts, and it's our job to identify those, cultivate them, and share them in the community. The goal is not only to contribute but to have a good time doing it. You want to get up in the morning feeling like you're really expressing yourself in the workplace, doing good work and making a difference.

Once you've clarified your motivated skills and area of interest, you'll be able to answer the perennial question "What are you looking for?" And the answer should be as simple as "I'm looking for a marketing job in wind power." This tells your audience the function you want to perform or the main skill you're offering (marketing) and the industry you're interested in (wind power).

The simplest way to transition to a green career is to take what you're already doing and apply to the green sector in which you're most interested. This is what I call the path of least resistance. For example, I was doing career consulting with executives who had been laid off when I decided that I wanted to have a green career. So I decided to use my career consulting skills to support people in transitioning to green careers. I stayed in the same function (career consulting), using skills I enjoy, but I changed the focus of my work to green careers.

Whatever function you're currently doing—human resources, finance, accounting, administration—you can do in a green company. There's a good chance that you'll be able to keep your salary the same or better, and you'll be able to hit the ground running, because you'll be doing the job function that you're already experienced in. You'll be an attractive candidate because employers usually look for people with experience in the function for which they're hiring.

Another way to think about a green career is to explore opportunities for work in your community. A major aspect of the move toward sustainability is "localization." We need to decentralize the economy and source our goods and services locally. Look around and see what's needed in your community: a good vegetarian restaurant, a green office supply store, an organic ice cream parlor, a fair trade organic coffee shop, ecological dry cleaners, a bicycle sales and maintenance shop, and so forth. There are many basic goods and services that most communities lack. So if you have an entrepreneurial bent and would like to start up a local business, there's opportunity all around you. If you're not yearning to start your own business, then look and see who is already doing something related to your interests and join them.

Local governments have become attractive employers for green job seekers. City and county governments are becoming the leaders in sustainability initiatives, partly because our federal government is doing so little. For example, the San Francisco Department of the Environment (sfenvironment.org) is leading the country in many ways with innovative programs to reduce waste, promote urban organic agriculture, transform waste cooking oil into fuel for city vehicles, encourage green building practices, and move toward renewable energy. The City of Berkeley has an initiative to pay for the initial cost of installing solar panels on homes and stretching out the payments over time by adding a small amount to the homeowners' property taxes. Salt Lake City is trapping the methane that comes off its garbage dump and sewage treatment plant, and burning it to create electricity that powers those facilities.

Cities are stepping up to the plate, largely due to grassroots pressure, because we citizens have the most access and leverage at the local level. City governments tend to pay well, too. In the old days, when you thought of city government, you would think, "Oh, no, the bureaucracy." But now city governments are attracting some of the best and brightest people who see the opportunity to make a big difference. There is a lot of leverage to be had at the local government level. So start checking the websites of city and county governments.

The Importance of Networking

Networking is the most effective strategy for job hunting. Most jobs are never advertised, and yet people make the mistake of assuming that the job listings are an accurate indication of what's available. Nothing could be farther from the truth. Staring at the want ads in the paper or on the Internet is depressing and usually not fruitful. Most jobs are filled through networking. The main reason to look at green job openings is to identify employers who may be interesting companies for you to approach.

Many people are terrified of the "N" word: *networking*. All it means is contacting everyone you know to tell them what you're looking for and ask for their ideas about potential employers and contacts. You can activate your network by sending a broadcast e-mail to your friends, family, and colleagues saying, "OK, folks, here's what I'm looking for (function and industry) and here are a list of employers I'm interested in. Do you know anyone who works in these organizations, or can you suggest other organizations in this industry for me to contact?" LinkedIn is an excellent resource for networking. Invite everyone in your network to join you on LinkedIn, and then you'll have access to their networks. You can also search by company name to see if you have any contacts in your extended network.

So how do you find green organizations in your area of interest? Co-op America's National Green Pages (greenpages.org) is an excellent resource, or go online to greenfestivals.org and check out the Green Festival exhibitors (over 400 green employers) in your area of interest.

The next step is to see if you can set up informational interviews at your target organizations. This is easier if you can use your network to identify people to approach, but it can be done without contacts, too. If it is a small organization, go right to the director. If it's a large organization, see if you can identify a person in charge of the functional area that you are interested in and send an e-mail. You can call the company, get the e-mail address of the person you want to connect with, send that person an e-mail saying that you have these skills and experience (attach a résumé), and see if you can get 20 minutes of his or her time to have a phone conversation.

Think creatively about how you can engage with the people in your area of interest. By networking and informational interviewing, you'll build a network in your new career area and increase your knowledge of the opportunities there. With persistence, a positive attitude, and some luck, you'll find what you're looking for. So take that next step toward a green career and be part of the new frontier.

Green Collar Jobs

Green collar jobs are blue-collar jobs in green businesses; that is, manual labor jobs in businesses whose products and services directly improve environmental quality. Green collar jobs are located in large and small for-profit businesses, non-profit organizations, social enterprises, and public sector institutions. What unites these jobs is that all of them are associated with manual labor work that directly improves environmental quality.

Green collar jobs represent an important new category of workforce opportunities because they are relatively high quality jobs, with relatively low barriers to entry, in sectors that are poised for dramatic growth. The combination of these three features means that cultivating green collar jobs for people with barriers to employment can be an effective strategy to provide low-income men and women with access to good jobs - jobs that provide workers with meaningful, community serving work, living wages, benefits, and advancement opportunities.

Twenty-two different sectors of the U.S. economy currently provide workers with green collar jobs. These sectors include:

1. Bicycle repair and bike delivery services
2. Car and truck mechanic jobs, production jobs, and gas-station jobs related to bio-diesel, vegetable oil and other alternative fuels
3. Energy retrofits to increase energy efficiency and conservation
4. Food production using organic and/or sustainably grown agricultural products
5. Furniture making from environmentally certified and recycled wood
6. Green building
7. Green waste composting on a large scale

8. Hauling and reuse of construction and demolition materials and debris
9. Hazardous materials clean up
10. Green (sustainable) landscaping
11. Manufacturing jobs related to large-scale production of a wide range of appropriate technologies (i.e. solar panels, bike cargo systems, green waste bins, etc.)
12. Materials reuse/producing products made from recycled, non-toxic materials
13. Non-toxic household cleaning in residential and commercial buildings
14. Parks and open space maintenance and expansion
15. Printing with non-toxic inks and dyes and recycled papers
16. Public transit jobs
17. Recycling
18. Solar installation and maintenance
19. Tree cutting and pruning
20. Peri-urban and urban agriculture
21. Water retrofits to increase water efficiency and conservation
22. Whole home performance (i.e.: HVAC, attic insulation, weatherization, etc.)

This piece is taken from *Green Collar Jobs: An Analysis of the Capacity of Green Businesses to Provide High Quality Jobs for Men and Women with Barriers to Employment* by Raquel Pinderhughes. The full report can be found at bss.sfsu.edu/raquelrp/. For more information, contact Raquel Pinderhughes at raquelrp@sfsu.edu.

Accelerating the Shift
to Green Energy

Jerome Ringo

Jerome Ringo is the immediate past chair of the five million–member National Wildlife Federation and is currently the national president of the Apollo Alliance, a coalition of trade unions and environmental groups pushing the federal government for massive investments in renewable energy and green job training.

My father was a civil rights worker, and he fought to help integrate the schools in Louisiana. My brothers and I were the guinea pigs. I was the first African American at the middle school. But the night before school, my father woke us up at 2 A.M., brought us to the front of the room, and we looked out the window, and there were two truckloads of Klansmen burning a cross in our front yard.

I grew up in Louisiana, worked in the petrochemical industry for a polluting company for about 22 years, blew the whistle on that company, and worked very diligently to organize communities on the other side of the fence line. It was part of our standard operating procedure that we discharged at night so that we would not be caught by the enforcement agencies in Louisiana because they got off duty at 11 P.M. It bothered me because we would discharge benzene hexachloride, dioxins, chlorines—you name it. If we needed to discharge a container, we would dump it into the ditch. Though it was illegal, we did it. Often I would watch the chemicals as they would roll down the ditch away from our plant, under our fence line, into the yards of nearby poor communities. Those communities were inhabited by people who looked very much like me.

It was difficult to sleep at night, knowing that in the plant where I worked, we were protected. OSHA required that we wore protective clothing to keep us from being burned in the plant; we wore respirators to keep us from being exposed to gases; we wore monitors that would tell us when we were in contact with hydrogen sulfide. I have often wondered, "Why were people just across the fence not given the same protection?" Those people who were poor and lived in dilapidated housing did not have much education. They did not get the luxury of protective clothing or respirators. I missed many nights of sleep because of this.

I made a decision to go out and organize those people across that fence line and help them understand what was going on. In 1989, I helped the community fight my company's permit, while still working for the company. That mixed like oil and water. Later that year, just before the permit was issued, the company called me in and said, "We're going to transfer you to Malaysia." I didn't return 'til years later.

When I returned, I was determined to dedicate my life to fighting for those people on the other side of the fence. I joined the Louisiana Wildlife Federation in 1991. At that time, the Louisiana Wildlife Federation was the largest environmental organization in the state; it had about 24,000 members. When I joined, I was the only black member. Today, the organization's membership has fallen to about 19,000. And today, I am the only black member.

What I found in Louisiana, as well as in the rest of this country, is that the conservation movement lacked diversity, and there was a lack of involvement of women, people of color, or the poor. I worked my way up through the Louisiana Wildlife Federation, became its vice president, and then joined the National Wildlife Federation, ran for the board of directors, served on that board for 10 years, and eventually became chairman of the board. That organization with its five million members lacked diversity as well. I came to the realization that it was not because the conservation organizations were racist;.it was not because they were elitists; there were many other reasons. Much of the reason rested within the neighborhoods across the fence line.

Poor people are more concerned with next month's rent. The melting of the glaciers on Mount Kilimanjaro is not an issue for low-income Americans. So I set out on a mission to help diversify the conservation movement by helping poor people and people of color rework their list of priorities so habitat destruction and depletion of the ozone layer are just as important as next month's rent.

Organizations must establish common ground with exploited communities and meet those communities where they are. Groups need to find out what the key issues are in the community and how they can work on the issues that impact daily life in those communities.

How do we make energy affordable for poor people who use less energy than the rich but pay a higher price than the rich? How can we level that playing field?

That brings me to the topic of energy. The Apollo Alliance is an organization made up of labor (the AFL-CIO, the United

Farmworkers, the Steelworkers), together with conservation organizations like the Sierra Club, the National Wildlife Federation, and Greenpeace. Ten years ago, it would have been unheard of for these groups to sit at the same table and talk openly about the issues. But now these organizations have come together: labor and conservation, the faith community, and the civil rights community. People from all walks of life have come together around one common issue: ending our dependence on fossil fuels and pursuing alternative energy, and the many economic benefits attached to green-collar job creation.

Some years ago I was speaking on the steps of the U.S. Capitol against drilling in the arctic wildlife refuge. In the audience were several board members of the Apollo Alliance, and they were looking for a national president. They approached me because I had a diverse background. I had worked in industry, in conservation, and I was African American. So they hired me as their national president.

There was no need for me to come up with a new road map to build a diverse coalition around clean energy, because there were several instances in our history that gave us a road map. Dr. Martin Luther King Jr. had a recipe; he was able to turn civil rights battles into a broad national movement. He did that by building a coalition of whites, blacks, poor people, rich people, Jews, Catholics, Protestants, labor, and conservation groups. People from all walks of life came together around the common issue of civil rights.

The Galvanizing Issue of Our Time

Today we have an issue that has the potential to be the galvanizing issue of our time. That issue is global warming. Global warming impacts the lives of everyone on this Earth. It matters not the color of your skin, how much money you have, your culture, or your background; we are all affected.

The Apollo Alliance brings to the table a galvanizing solution. If we invest enough in the research and development of new energy alternatives, we can reduce the impact of global warming, reduce our dependency on foreign oil, reduce pollution, generate good clean jobs, and strengthen the U.S. economy.

Imagine when Hurricane Katrina hit the Gulf Coast and shut down the oil wells if, at the same time, the Middle Eastern countries from which we import so much of our oil also cut off their oil. America would have been brought to its knees. We must come up with innovative ideas as to how we can diversify our energy portfolio so our dependence on energy is not so lopsided.

The other benefit of alternative energy is that we are going to create a new green economy. We at Apollo believe that through research and development and the promotion of alternative energy, we can create 3 million new jobs in 10 years and promote more than $300 billion in new investment.

The reason we call it "Apollo" is because in 1961, President John F. Kennedy made a commitment to this country that we would put a person on the moon within 10 years. Well, we didn't do it in 10; we did it in 9. With the same energy and passion that it took for America to put a man on the moon (Project Apollo), we believe that in 10 years we can declare energy independence from foreign oil, we can stimulate the American economy and create a new green economy, and we can reduce carbon dioxide into the atmosphere and reduce the impacts of global warming.

We're living in a time when we have a sense of urgency in addressing issues of our economy and how we do business with respect to energy. There's a sense of urgency in addressing carbon sequestration, in fixing the assembly lines of Detroit. We have no time to argue. It's time for action.

In America today, we have got to reactivate activism. We've got to bring people to the table from all walks of life and build an alliance that is going to change the face of America and push aside our differences. We've got to come together as a nation around a common issue that is going to put the people of Detroit back to work, that is going to green the buildings of New York City, and that is going to hold presidential candidates accountable if they don't think and act green. We have a responsibility and an opportunity today to say to Congress—because of the billions of dollars that are going to be put in a big pot as a result of carbon auctioning and carbon trading—"We've got to make sure that it doesn't just stimulate the economy for *some* people, but it's a pathway out of poverty for *all*."

We've got to use our labor unions and community colleges to train people in green economy skills. We've got to stimulate the pockets of the labor unions to help them develop programs that will train people to build and maintain wind turbines and solar panels and build more efficient transportation systems.

One of the major components of the Apollo Alliance is business. Businesses are ultimately going to make the investments. We've got to create incentives to help businesses get going on this green path. Billions of dollars will be made from carbon trading, and it should be invested in helping new green businesses. In Louisiana, where the petrochemical industry is king, any new petroleum company that opens has a 10-year tax exemption. But if Mom and Pop want to open an organic grocery store on the corner, they have to pay taxes from day 1. What's wrong with that picture?

Some oil companies fear that if we reduce our dependence on fossil fuels, we are going to put people out of work. Well, why not take those same people and train them to do green jobs?

The Apollo Alliance is advocating training, training, training, and financing that training through existing entities like labor unions and community colleges, to create new jobs for America. Many in Congress are supporting the idea and are pushing it forward through federal legislation.

We now have at least 11 states that have passed renewable energy portfolio standards. In Pennsylvania, for example, Governor Ed Rendell passed a bill that is going to require that 18 or 19 percent of all energy produced in Pennsylvania be alternative energy. As a result, a Spanish company that builds wind turbines moved their operation to Pennsylvania and created 1,000 new jobs.

This is an opportunity for us to bring jobs back to America. I see nothing wrong with some American jobs being in other places; that's just the way of the world. But we've got too many people on the street corners of this country who are missing out on golden opportunities to improve their quality of life because we are sending so many good jobs out of our country. It's time for this country to regain respect as a productive nation. It's time for America to be America again.

We have to develop a very diversified energy portfolio so that when we have the next Katrina, we're not caught over the oil barrel. As I said to the Bush administration at the climate change negotiations in Montreal two years ago, "Down in Louisiana, we are suffering from category 5 storms, and the folks on Pennsylvania Avenue, when it comes to global warming and clean energy, are suffering from category 5 denial." Many in this country, unfortunately, are suffering from category 5 denial. There's no time for that.

We've got to have an Apollo moon-shot mission to stimulate the American economy.

It's really a challenge when I speak internationally, when people ask, "How can you tell China and India to curb their carbon emissions, when you, the United States, have not even ratified Kyoto?" And my response is "The position of the White House is not the position of the American people." If you don't think so, look at the actions of the U.S. Conference of Mayors and the National Governors Association and many green organizations around the country that are saying that the White House may be in denial, but we are going to take the necessary steps to stimulate our economy and create new green jobs.

Right now, the Earth is in critical condition, and you and I are the life support. What are we going to do? Right now, our economies are in critical condition. We have an opportunity through the Apollo Alliance and the programs we are promoting in the states across this country. You see Congress talking about a federal renewable portfolio standard. It is the grassroots, within the cities and the states of the National Council of Mayors and the National Governor's Association, that are going to drive federal policy and are going to drive federal policy makers to do the right thing. We have a great opportunity now. We have a Congress that has changed. With a new face in the White House, we have a huge opportunity.

One of our most important constituencies is our young people. We have to reach our kids because they are the future leaders of this country. They are going to be the ones who reactivate activism in this country. Remember during the civil rights movement, it was the young people who turned that movement around. I believe that it will be the young people who do the same with climate change.

The most critical elements to the success of a new green movement are you and me. Let us do as was done in the civil rights movement and the women's movement, and put aside our differences, gather around one common goal and belief, with passion, and drive the new green economy movement forward, and we can all reap the benefits.

Creating Green
Worker Cooperatives

OMAR FREILLA

*Omar Freilla created the Green Worker Cooperative to turn
the mountains of New York City garbage trucked through the
South Bronx into jobs for the community.*

I'm from the South Bronx, the poorest congressional district
in the country. It has 24 percent unemployment, which is
incredibly high, especially when you think New York City's
rate is about 5 to 7 percent.

For the past three and a half years, I have been working to
create what we at Green Worker Cooperatives feel is the beginning of an alternative green economy, based on empowering
workers, so that the people of our community are able to live
and work in a place where they can decide their own fate and do
it in a way that improves the environmental conditions in the
South Bronx.

The South Bronx has been a dumping ground for much of
New York City, as lots of neighborhoods around the country,
like the South Side of Chicago, are used as dumping grounds.

Places like the South Bronx are turned into dumping grounds because every time waste is thrown out the door from some place, it comes to some place that is usually a poor, working-class neighborhood, and a community of color.

The biggest thing we export in New York City is garbage. New York City produces about 50,000 tons of garbage every day that winds up moving through two neighborhoods: the South Bronx and Williamsburg Green Point. Both are poor working-class neighborhoods. In the South Bronx, we have waste facilities that are huge lots where garbage is dumped, processed, and then sent out in large trailer trucks. We have sewage sludge processing plants. There's a waste water treatment plant right next to a smokestack and numerous other types of facilities—junk shops, many power plants, things that nobody really thinks about but that have disastrous impacts on the neighborhoods.

That these facilities usually wind up in these neighborhoods is no accident. Much of what determines where the polluting facilities get built is whether the people who live there are able to resist, and that is based on class and race. If you have resources that enable you to get a lawyer or a design group that puts together posters and flyers, if you have access to the press, these things are based on your social contacts and your money.

Our small neighborhood has about 11,000 people and that many truck trips, coming in and out of the neighborhood. So there are horrible odors that waft through the entire neighborhood and an incredible problem with high rates of respiratory illnesses. It has one of the highest rates of asthma in the country.

Because of these conditions, over the years we have learned how to fight, how to wage campaigns against companies doing us harm. But now we want to channel our energy into creating clean jobs that help us and the environment. We don't want the dirty jobs that are contaminating our communities. We want an alternative.

We want to shut down the waste transfer stations and the sewage sludge processing plant. But the people working there, in the dirtiest jobs, live in our neighborhood. So, we need to create new jobs for them if we are going to shut down the polluting facilities. It is not enough to shut those down; we need to create better ones.

We started Green Worker Cooperatives because we wanted to create jobs that provide green alternatives. If we created an opportunity to reuse each piece of brick, drywall, kitchen cabinet, material that flows through one of these waste facilities, we could create an incredible amount of work for people in the community. When we do that, we will be reducing waste, creating new jobs, preserving natural resources, and keeping more trees standing.

In New York, when a building is torn down, everything that is ripped out is thrown into a huge dumpster in front of the building: kitchen cabinets, hardwood floors, sheetrock, lumber, bricks, everything. That stuff is trucked to the South Bronx, thrown onto the ground, and a dust suppression device, which is basically one guy standing at the corner with a garden hose, spraying water on this huge mound of rubble. Then a tractor comes over, and it moves over it repeatedly, picks it all up, and dumps it into a long tractor trailer. That trailer gets trucked out to Ohio or Virginia, to another poor working-class community. It is dumped into a hole in the ground.

The Green Institute in Minneapolis runs a place called the ReUse Center. This is like a Home Depot for used stuff, all kinds of building materials. S. Oregon, founded in 1999, is along the same lines and started by a nonprofit. There's ReCycle North in Burlington, Vermont, and Urban Ore in Berkeley,

California, which has been around almost 30 years. They're all remaking building materials that normally get thrown out.

Over the past four years, we have been laying the ground-work to start our own building materials reuse store: It's called ReBuilders Source, and it's a retail warehouse for salvaged and surplus building materials.

We really had no idea what we were doing but knew that we wanted to create work locally and build a movement that was about green-collar jobs and could really create hope. Those of us fighting environmental justice fights want to say that we don't need anymore transfer stations; we don't need any of these things we are told are going to create jobs.

The Institute for Local Self Reliance released a study a few years ago that looked at whether you can create jobs out of the quest for reducing waste. They found that for every job in the waste industry, you could create as many as 10 to 250 jobs depending on whether you were doing recycling or reusing that "waste." For every job where someone throws a computer into a hole in the ground, you can create dozens of jobs training and teaching people how to refurbish computers and put them back into circulation.

For us, it is not enough just to say that we have a green job. We want to create them. Being green for us is really social, envi-ronmental justice. It's making sure that people who are working in these places are not exploited.

It's not green if you don't consider the people living right across the street or the people working there. Are the people who work in the recycling plant benefiting?

We started the Green Worker Co-op Academy as a way to spread the word in our community about worker ownership and green-collar jobs. We have put people through training where we show them how money moves in the neighborhood. If most of the stores are chain stores, the ownership is not local. In a place like the South Bronx, money comes in, and it goes right back out again.

It makes no sense to buy into the old argument that if you wanted to create a new society, you need to take state power and become the state. With the fall of the Soviet Union, we recognize that we need to deal with the economy where we live. We need to create an alternative to it and recognize that the alternative has to be one that empowers every single one of us and doesn't leave us at the hands of a state in the same way that it doesn't leave us at the hands of some megacorporation.

One way to do that is to create an economy based on worker ownership. We really feel that it creates accountability. For those of us in the environmental justice movement, we say that any decision that affects a community, whether it is South Bronx or Little Village or Pilsen or any other working-class community of color, needs to be decided by us, not by government agencies or even large mainstream environmental organizations.

What would happen if the executives in that sewage sludge processing plant lived in the neighborhood or if the smokestack were turned around and went into the boardroom? Would they be allowing pollution to go untreated into the air or the water as they are doing right now? I would say no.

Then there is the issue of money. A lot of us have an aversion to dealing with money; if you are on the left, you feel money is evil and need to not talk about it. That somehow that makes us righteous. But if you ignore it, then you allow whatever happens to continue. It is not enough to just look the other way. You still go to stores. It is still something that you use.

There are plenty of people who want money. They want money to feed themselves, feed their families, to be able to go on a vacation, to cover their health needs, to do all kinds of things. So when we say that we have issues with money, I think what we are really saying is we have issues with ownership. We have issues with the use of money.

We have this incredible disparity of wealth. How do you create a situation where everyone in the community actually has wealth? You create a structure where you don't have someone making 100 times or 1,000 times what the lowest-paid person makes. You can't do that in a business setup where everyone is an owner. I don't think there is anyone here that would feel comfortable with any other person making 100 or a 1,000 times what they make. So it creates accountability, an equalizing structure. If 10 people working in a cooperative have profits at the end of the year, that profit is distributed among the 10 people who are working there. Each time that that happens, those 10 people are more likely to go to their corner grocery store. They are shopping at the supermarket in their community. Their money is staying in their community and cycling much more often than is the case right now.

On another level, it's being able to have the basic empowerment of having a say in your own reality and do what for most of us in this country is the impossible: to say, "I experience democracy on a day-to-day basis."

Who are we to talk about democracy and the value and imperative of voting? To say that this is a democratic society and these are democratic values? We don't even know what democracy looks like. If that's so, then we are in no position to preach democracy to anybody else. I think the very first thing is that we start experiencing democracy and know what democracy looks like on a day-to-day basis. If you are making decisions that affect your own life on a day-to-day basis, at least once a week, then you can start to say, "I know what democracy is, and I can talk to you about democracy."

I had never been part of a co-op, and then one day, I decided I was going to start an incubator for co-ops. I hadn't even seen a co-op. I had heard of them and thought, "That sounds like a good idea." Some of us got together and said, "This is what we are going to do." We created our own model, which only time will tell if it actually works. Green Worker Cooperatives is a nonprofit organization, and the co-ops that we are creating are initially partnerships between Green Worker and the workers. We created our own structure, which I am told is new. We have created the co-ops as LLCs—limited liability companies—with two partners, one being our nonprofit organization and the other being the workers who are separately incorporated as a cooperative. So, the workers are coming in organized, together, as a cooperative, and we are coming in as a partner. In our structure, over time, we phase ourselves out as the nonprofit, and the workers become more empowered, and it becomes a 100 percent worker-owned cooperative.

Our process for phasing ourselves out is that everybody learns the basics of finance and accounting, business structures, and how to actually do strategic planning. Those are the skills we have. We are starting our first one with four people. Our collective starts with four, and it will grow to 20 or 30 or 40, and so that skill level has to be built up over time.

Our website is greenworker.coop. If you want to learn more about worker cooperatives in general, I would recommend that you check out the website of the United States Federation of Worker Cooperatives, which is usworker.coop.

There is a growing movement that I see happening within the United States. We are finally starting to catch up with a lot of the movements that are happening in other parts of the world.

PART FOUR

Greening Your Home, Community, and Planet

Creating Healthy Homes

DAVID JOHNSTON

If you had to pick a handful of people who have been most responsible for moving this country toward green building practices, David Johnston would be among those few. He is not only an experienced residential builder himself—he knows how to hammer a nail straight—but he also understands the politics of promoting the green building industry. His book is titled Green Remodeling.

I have been doing green building work since before there was a name "green building." In fact, I got a degree in what was called passive solar. After I got my degree, it was called applied climatology for a while. We are still in the process of applying climatology; the only difference is we have a changing climate. So we have to apply the science in a different way.

Those of you who own your home are probably going to do something to change your indoor climate. You might make your doors bigger, your rooms bigger, or your house bigger. Everything you do has to be done with consciousness. What I would like to do in this essay is explain why and how to consciously change your home, no matter what you are doing, because every aspect of your home and every product you bring into your home is a vote for whether your children have the same options that we did—or not.

If you have children, you need to think of them when you think about green building. They are the ones who are going to pay the price for what we have done to this planet. As builders in the early 1980s, we did not think twice about things like indoor air quality. We didn't know. I exposed myself, my crews, and my subcontractors to some of the most toxic materials in the marketplace. We know better now.

This country has not built a sustainable building since Native Americans erected the last tepees. The only truly sustainable buildings are igloos or the pueblos in New Mexico and Arizona. Everything else is just building in a way that is slightly less environmentally problematic than we have traditionally been doing for the last 60 years. A green building can look like anything, it can be anywhere, and it does not fall into a singular category. I came out of the solar industry, and in those days back in the early 1980s, *solar-ugly* was one word. Now, *green-ugly* does not have to be one word; it can look like anything, it can be any place, but it does everything differently. It is much more energy-efficient; it uses resources in the highest and best use possible, providing a healthy living environment.

Green building has become mainstream because of public demand. People have demanded green building; the government has not funded it. Big business has come into it kicking and screaming. It is a phenomenon that began in the San Francisco Bay Area, and it is spreading more quickly in California than anywhere else in the country. It is because Californians are voting with their wallets, and that is a key to changing this system.

Ten years ago, we thought we knew who our market was: they shopped at Whole Foods, belonged to Greenpeace, did yoga, meditated. Yet market research over the past decade tells us that is not who is demanding it. It is all over Middle America: red states and blue states. Market research tells us that people who bought green homes were not necessarily involved in the environmental movement. In a survey we did in Colorado, only 10 percent of green homebuyers were involved with environmental groups. They did not shop at Whole Foods, did not do yoga. But six months after they moved into a green home, guess what? Half of them started shopping at Whole Foods, joined environmental groups, or started meditating. That is why more and more people are buying green: it is healthier, it is more efficient, it is quieter, it is safer, it is more durable, and it has a better environmental impact.

A growing number of people are not comfortable with the standard toxic home. Seventy-four percent of people we surveyed said they were not getting the energy and environmental features they wanted. What if 74 percent of your customers said, "You are not giving me what I want"? What would you do? You'd change something, right? Well, that is what is happening in the home building industry. They must change their product because you are telling them, "Take your plastic disposable house and shove it—I deserve something better; I demand something better." That is one of the basic ways we change things in a capitalist society.

Why are buildings so important? Because buildings are responsible for 40 percent of energy used worldwide. We cannot talk about sustainability without changing the building sector. I liked to call it "bringing sustainability home to where people live."

So, we mold our environment and our environment molds us. It is our intention with green building to really do both at the same time.

We Americans are less than 5 percent of the world's population, yet we are using 25 percent of world's resources. So we have to change faster than anybody, because we have a greater impact than anybody. And one area of our greatest impact is in how we get wood and paper. All around the world, we clear-cut forests in order to get these products. Over 95 percent of U.S. forests have been logged to date. When we clear-cut a forest, we fundamentally change the ecosystem. And when we change the microbial ecology in the soil, we damage nature's ability to sustain life.

So what we do about all this? First of all, when we are talking about energy, a typical builder is going to say, "Mr. and Mrs. Jones, I am going to build your house to code." What does that really mean? It is a bare minimum; it means that if you built any worse, it would be illegal. We need to be 50 percent better than the energy code to begin with. With regard to insulation, any time you change an outer wall, you should put as much insulation in there as you can, because the future is completely uncertain about energy prices.

There are alternatives to wood, and there are alternative sources of wood. For example, bamboo, which is actually a grass, only takes 3 to 5 years to grow until it is big enough to harvest and turn into flooring. It takes 40 to 60 years for an oak tree or a cherry tree to mature in order to be turned into a floor. Additionally, there is the possibility of reclaiming wood. There are countless wooden beams coming down from old warehouses. There is stunning heart redwood and clear heart fir being turned into furniture. There is a huge market for these salvaged resources.

Is Your Home Killing You?

Something we do not hear in the news is that, of the hundreds of chemicals regulated by the Environmental Protection Agency, only two are more prevalent outside than inside our homes. We've done so much worrying about smog and power plants, while ignoring the fact that pollution is worse inside most of our homes than it is outside. This issue is the sleeping giant in the building industry.

When it comes to indoor air quality, it's all about the microparticulates—not the stuff you see in a beam of sunlight coming through the window; it's the things you don't see—such as asbestos and fiberglass insulation—that are the problem. Composition gases are also a problem. Whether it is a water heater, a furnace, or a gas stove, we are not venting those gases outside our homes effectively, and when we turn on an exhaust fan or the dryer, it can cause carbon monoxide poisoning and other kinds of respiratory disease from breathing the unburned gases.

Volatile organic compounds (VOCs) are the insidious ones. These are the "enes": gasoline, kerosene, and benzene. Other chemicals like formaldehyde are much more prevalent, but they all come under this category of VOCs. If you use a tube of adhesive or a can of paint, a finish for a wood floor, it is going to have "TVOC" in grams per liter on it. It means total VOC, and you want to look at every can you open. Make sure that those total VOCs are less than 100, preferably less than 50. There are many great products on the market now that are zero VOC, which is the best.

Lead paint is another issue. People painted with lead paint up until 1978. So be careful if you are replacing windows, filling cracks, and chipping away old paint. You may be releasing poisonous lead paint dust that is easy to accidentally ingest. Lead test kits are cheap and easy to use.

Moisture and mold can be an issue when the environment changes from being more humid inside to more humid outside. Moisture pressure always wants to equalize, and it does this through the walls. We need to really pay attention to how weather-tight our buildings are when we are remodeling, and watch for things like drainage planes, and how water runs off the outside of the building. We want the walls to dry to the inside if water gets into the wall cavity between the studs.

There is an excellent program in California called Build It Green that offers green remodeling guidelines, available for free from builditgreen.org or stopwaste.org. These sites give you very specific things to talk to your contractor about—what products to use, how you can do it, how to think about it. Look for a local green building program that will give you guidance on green building in your immediate area.

So, the fundamental question before we get into one room at a time is "How much?" Everybody thinks that the answer is "Too much." That is part of the mythology. If you own a house, you know that everything comes down to Principal, Interest, Taxes, and Insurance. P-I-T-I is the equation your mortgage banker uses to calculate how much you can afford to pay. In the green building world, we add an E-W to that P-I-T-I for your monthly Energy and Water bills. The real issue is energy. If you put those six figures together, your monthly net is typically going to be less after a green remodel than if you did a conventional remodel, because your energy bills should be considerably lower than the monthly cost of your second mortgage loan.

How about indoor air quality—protecting your children from asthma? What is that investment worth to you? The great thing about most of the indoor air quality improvements is that they don't cost very much. In fact, in some cases it is actually the same price for a gallon of paint that has no chemicals as one that does.

Affordability is a different way of thinking from just first costs, and green building is about thinking how we can make an investment in the future.

So, let's take one room at a time, beginning with bathrooms. I've remodeled hundreds of bathrooms and have found several recurring problems. One common issue has to do with plumbing and the loss of heat. You need to get the plumbing out of the exterior walls so that you are not losing heat through pipes that run through empty cavity walls. Insulating hot water pipes is an easy way to save money instantly.

If you are remodeling the bathroom and reinsulating the walls, put half an inch or an inch of rigid foam on the inside if you have room. It will keep the moisture out of the wall cavities, and give you an extra weather barrier that reduces drafts, and make your bathroom warmer. When do you want to be most comfortable? When you're wet and naked, right?

Insulate built-in tubs. Just fill that cavity with insulation all the way around the tub. You want the tub to stay warm when you are in it. The area where the drain pipe goes down through the floor usually has an empty hole that goes right through the crawl space (the coldest area in the house) and comes up and cools the hottest thing in the house—which is your bath tub when you're in it.

On-demand hot water circulation pumps are a great technology. Instead of a constantly circulating hot water system, these pumps send water down the cold water pipe and back to the hot water, so that when you turn the faucet on, the water is instantly hot, and you don't have to let the water run to warm up. It saves water and saves energy at the same time.

With regard to your toilets, you can get rid of the 5- or 6-gallon flushers and put in 1.6-gallon toilet. You can get low-flow faucets and showerheads. You don't need a contractor to do the last one—you can do it immediately.

You want light in your bathrooms. The more light you have in the bathroom, the better your day will go. You'll wake up happier. You can use skylights, windows, or daylighting, a tubular skylight that can bring sunlight into parts of your home not accessible to a traditional skylight. Compact fluorescent bulbs use one-quarter as much energy as conventional lighting. LED lights use even less energy, and this technology is improving rapidly.

Our bodies are fundamentally wired for fresh air and natural daylight. If we deprive ourselves of those two things, our bodies will feel the ill effects. Natural daylight and ventilation are absolutely key. Day lighting makes all the difference in the world. I do not have to turn on the light in my home or in my office if the sun is out because I have large superglass windows and insulated skylights that bring sunlight into my home office, and everybody loves coming to meetings there, because it just feels good.

If you are building new walls, at a minimum try to use cellulose insulation rather than fiberglass. Cellulose is recycled wood fiber—agricultural waste. It is nontoxic, resource-efficient, and it is better insulation material. If you're using wood, make sure it is Forest Stewardship Council (FSC) certified and is sustainably harvested.

Heating and cooling is an area where huge cost savings are possible. My 1,000-square-foot office in Colorado uses a water heater to heat the entire building. If you build your roof and walls right, that is all you need. You do not need to put in big mechanical systems.

In closing, some things cost more, some things cost less, but you want to invest in the things of greater value. You want to invest in those things that are going to give you a more secure energy future. Look at the big picture. If you are going to remodel your home, you are probably going to stay there for a while. So, think about the 5-year horizon, the 10-year horizon. How much will energy cost then? It will save you increasing amounts of money as costs rise. Every penny you put into insulation will save you dollars and the cost of energy over time.

Most of all, please remember that ultimately, we did not inherit the Earth from our parents; we are merely borrowing it from our children.

Where's the Power?

FRANCES MOORE LAPPÉ

Frances Moore Lappé is the founder of the Small Planet Institute and author of the best-selling Diet for a Small Planet *and many other books, her most recent being* Getting a Grip: Clarity, Creativity and Courage in a World Gone Mad.

Beneath all the huge challenges facing our world is our widespread feeling of powerlessness. So, the most important question of our time may be "What robs us of power?"

Some may think the answer is Monsanto, Exxon, or the Far Right's influence in Washington. But, at a deeper level, could it be the power of ideas we hold?

Human beings are creatures of the mind. For us, there is no unfiltered reality: We see and interpret our world through psychological lenses; we simply can't see that which doesn't fit within these mental maps. Now, this is all well and good if we're alive at a time when the dominant mental map is life serving. But, you and I are alive in an extraordinary moment: when the dominant mental map, now going global, is fundamentally life destroying.

The Premise of Scarcity

At the center of the prevailing mental map is the premise of scarcity: There are not enough goods, nor enough goodness. There's not enough *of anything*, be it food, or energy, or love . . . or parking places! And, even worse, there's not enough goodness in human nature to enable us to make the needed planetary turnaround.

With this premise of scarcity permeating everything, we come to believe that the only way to stay alive is to focus narrowly on the materialistic, self-centered, and competitive aspects of ourselves. Then, what happens? If we really believe we are merely this caricature of humanity, of course we can't trust ourselves to come together in common problem solving to address our planetary crises. In other words, democracy itself is suspect.

With no faith in ourselves, we look not to deliberation but for automatic laws and immutable forces to determine our fate. Ronald Reagan named one big one in the 1980s: the "magic of the market." So, whether it be school lunches or prisons, why not turn them over to the market's magic since we are too flawed to make real democracy work?

But what Reagan called magic boils down to *one* type of market driven by a single rule: the highest return to existing wealth. We come to believe that our way of life rests on two things joined at the hip: a one-rule economy plus elections. If we have these, then we're home free. We've got democracy we can export anywhere!

Thin Democracy

These assumptions lead inexorably to what we have today: a society in which the corporate executive, by noon on the first day in January, can earn as much as a minimum wage worker in America earns working all year. Such concentrated wealth inevitably infects and warps the political process. More than two dozen lobbyists roam the corridors of Washington for every official elected to represent us there.

Elections plus a one-rule economy are what I call "thin democracy," and it's dangerous. It neither brings out the best in us nor protects us from the worst. Thin democracy, by resulting in such extreme imbalances in human relationships, actually unleashes the worst: our willingness to brutalize one another. Surely, humanity has now learned: Concentrated human power makes cruelty inevitable, as we've seen from the Holocaust to Abu Ghraib.

Starting from the premise of lack, our belief system leads to deadly consequences: a downward spiral of powerlessness.

We will continue to grasp for straws, for any act of charity or protest, until we see how we got here and therefore how we can reverse the negative forces, creating a new, life-affirming cycle.

Thus, humanity's challenge today is to consciously birth a new life-serving thought system based on evidence of what elicits the best in us. But human beings don't just leap into a void. We don't jump ship; we must first be able to see a new way of understanding on the horizon before we can abandon a failing vessel.

Living Democracy

Fortunately, a more positive thought system is emerging. I call it "living democracy." It starts from the opposite premise: the premise of *possibility*. It drops the debate over the goodness "of" human nature and simply acknowledges the hard-wired positive capacities "in" human nature that we can tap. This very different premise leads to very different consequences.

Living democracy, rather than being softheaded, is what I call "heart-centered realism." It is based in evidence of what works. Democracy becomes not a set system we merely inherit but a set of system values we consciously use as guides in all aspects of our culture. One of those is fairness.

Think about it. During more than 90 percent of human social evolution, we lived in tightly woven tribes where our individual survival depended on the tribe's survival. We also learned that unfairness could destroy community cohesion; it is fair rules, fairly enforced, that hold community together. Even the supposed "Godfather of Greed" Adam Smith, a moral philosopher, said of humanity that, yes, we all share many social sentiments, but one is special: "We are in some peculiar manner tied, bound, and obliged to the observation of justice." He grasped that injustice utterly destroys community.

A sense of fairness shows up even beyond even the human species. Capuchin monkeys, scientists tell us, will throw back their rations to their keepers if they feel they're not getting a square deal. Scientists have also found through MRI studies that when human beings are cooperating, the same parts of our brains light up as when we eat chocolate—that's how pleasurable working together is.

Equally important is our hard-wired empathy. Scientists observe that babies cry at the sound of other babies crying, but not at a recording of their own cry. Rhesus monkeys have been shown to refrain for days from eating if they see that to eat they must pull a lever causing pain to another monkey. Surely we are not less empathetic than these monkeys!

In addition to our capacity for empathy and our sense of fairness, philosopher Erich Fromm stressed our innate need for efficacy: "our need to make a dent." Such a need is virtually universal, he argued. As Fromm put it, in a twist on

Descartes, the human essence could be summed up as "I am because I effect."

With these needs and capacities thwarted by thin democracy, no wonder depression is epidemic.

Now, living democracy isn't handed down to us. It is what we are cocreating, moment to moment.

It is a skills-based culture that is learned. To take just one example I encountered recently: In their own successful student-initiated course on ecological sustainability at the University of California–Santa Cruz, now with about 300 enrolled, the student organizers realized early on that they needed to learn communication skills to be able to pull off such a big challenge. They recognized that democracy is a process, an art; as you learn its skills you don't just divvy up power; you create new power.

Living democracy is not driven by highest return to existing wealth but by values rooted in our deep needs of fairness, inclusion, and mutual accountability. Thus, it is never finished but dynamic and always evolving.

Once we understand democracy as a culture that we create, we realize that its values work as just as well in economic and cultural life as in political life. We don't have to divide ourselves up and leave the best of ourselves at home, when we go into the public realm.

Let me give you some concrete examples that show what's possible.

Living Economies

Imagining democratic economics is often the biggest stumbling block. *New York Times* columnist Thomas Friedman wrote in a recent book, "[T]here is no more mint chocolate chip, there is no more strawberry swirl, there is no more lemon-lime. Today there is only free-market vanilla and North Korea."[1] In other words, since almost no one would choose top-down state control, all that's left is corporate capitalism. The problem is that too many, like Friedman, conflate capitalism and a market economy, when there are many brilliant ways to organize a market that are life serving. Think of Fair Trade. In the UK today, half of the population recognizes the Fair Trade label, and that's happened in no time, historically speaking. Citizens' choosing of Fair Trade has already lifted a million families out of poverty around the world. That's power shopping!

The Fair Trade movement is linked to the rapid expansion of democratic enterprises. But when many people hear the word *cooperative*, they think "quaint" and "marginal." Yet co-op membership has doubled in the last 30 years, and more people are members of cooperatives than own shares in publicly traded corporations. We're recognizing that cooperatives can create stunningly successful markets.

A year ago I had the privilege of wandering around Bologna, Italy, the home of perhaps one of the most interesting examples of a local living economy—almost 40 percent of the gross domestic product in this prosperous region of four million people is co-op generated. These enterprises tax themselves 3 percent of profits to maintain a financial pool supporting one another in marketing and financing. It is the net worth of these cooperatives that has made this region one of Italy's wealthiest.

Closer to home, in Ashland, Oregon, recently I was told that there are more food co-ops forming now than there were in the 1970s. They are also helping one another: The Ashland co-op helped the Medford co-op get started with a $10,000 grant.

Equally important is how we crack the dominant map that says; "It has all been globalized. It's all over."

How do we reclaim diverse ownership and more secure localized provisioning that makes sense for our planet and our bodies? I recently learned that, of the major food crops in the world that the UN counts, with the exception of oil, seeds, and fruit, almost 90 percent is still eaten in the country in which it is produced. A worldwide "food sovereignty" movement is growing. In 2007, in the West African country of Mali, 600 people from almost 100 countries gathered. Instead of putting people in a hotel, they created a village for participants to talk about how to put food for local people before exports. The Mali farmer organization hosting this gathering had just achieved a major policy victory for their country—one emphasizing food first for Malians.

In living democracy, government serves at least two critical roles: as a convener of problem solvers and also as an institution that sets fair rules. Living democracy does not require big government; it requires accountable government.

And one prerequisite to setting fair rules in living democracy is, of course, getting money out of the system. Unfortunately, a lot of Americans have totally given up on this goal. The best-kept secret in America—and one we need to energetically expose—may be that, at the state level, getting money out of the system is working. Marge Mead, a grandma in Arizona, walked into a League of Women Voters meeting in the 1990s and, discovering she was the only person who knew shorthand, volunteered to keep the minutes. She said, "That act turned out to begin my reincarnation as a political activist." And she became a leader in the Clean Elections campaign in Arizona that is already allowing more diverse people to run for office. Maine also passed a Clean Elections bill, starting with a 26-year-old political science grad who took it on.

In part because over 80 percent of Maine legislators now run for office with public money and no corporate money, that state recently passed producer responsibility legislation. It's big in Europe but just starting to catch on in the United States. Producer responsibility says to corporations, "You're responsible for the entire life cycle of your product." It is revolutionary. The Maine Natural Resources Council of Maine started it. They'd been moved by a film that showed workers in China dismantling our discarded electronics with all the lead and cadmium and mercury totally exposed, with no protection, and they said, "We've got to do something." So, they started campaigning for producer responsibility, and all the big computer and electronics companies came to Maine to oppose it. Hewlett-Packard was the only exception because it has created a plant to reuse and recycle. And the worst corporate offender? Apple.

But Maine legislators passed the legislation anyway. In the first five months, the corporations who made the electronics equipment reclaimed almost a million pounds of it. It was headed for landfills or export. They reused or recycled it.

Clearly, the Mainers who pushed ahead in this historic fight had guts. It takes real courage to speak out, to challenge the dominant mental map defending corporate-dominated thin democracy. So maybe the key to finding our power is rethinking fear itself.

Rethinking Fear

We humans evolved in tribes in which we understood two things: our hard-wired fear sensations, like the tight throat or the pounding heart, are reliable signals that tell us we're in danger. We also evolved knowing that to separate from the pack meant death.

But wait: What happens if now, in the early 21st century, the dominant pack, with its destructive economic system, is heading right over Victoria Falls? In that circumstance, separating from the pack would no longer mean death but *life*. But going against the dominant system still triggers fear sensations.

So perhaps the most important choice we make in our lives is how we respond to fear. Are we able to let go of the notion that fear is an ironclad verdict that we are wrong or in danger, and come to see fear as information? It may be telling us we are doing exactly what needs to be done, for ourselves and for our precious planet. I for one have learned that, whether nervous or outraged, I can choose to redefine the pounding of my heart as "inner applause."

In addition to a new boldness, we need a new humility.

Bold Humility

When I asked a founder of the Landless Workers Movement (MST) in Brazil, "What made you think you could create successful land reform when earlier attempts had failed?" he responded, "Possible? Success? We never thought of success, we just began. We knew we had to."

We see this stance in so many mass movements. People choose to act not by weighing their odds of success but because it is the only way to be fully alive themselves. They embody what I think of as empowering humility. They are saying by their actions that *it's not possible to know what's possible*, so we're free. We're free to go for the world we want.

Every time you demonstrate that the market is not some supernatural force, it is just a tool that we can use to realize our values, every time you reveal who you really are, admit your fear, and learn how to walk forward with a pounding heart, you are defeating a deadly belief system that tells us lies about ourselves. You are giving birth to *the heart-centered realism of living democracy*.

You have what all human beings want. You have purpose, meaning, and energy. That's *your power*. Glory in it.

Note

1. See Thomas L. Friedman, *The Lexus and the Olive Tree: Understanding Globalization* (New York: Anchor Books, 1999).

Top 10 Reasons to Support Locally Owned Enterprises

1. *Significantly more money recirculates in the local economy when purchases are made at locally owned, rather than nationally owned, businesses.* More money is kept in the community because locally owned businesses usually purchase from other local businesses, service providers, and farms.

2. *Nonprofits receive greater support.* Nonprofit organizations receive an average of three times greater support from smaller locally owned business owners than they do from large businesses.

3. *Our one-of-a-kind businesses are an integral part of our distinctive character.* The unique character of our community is what brought us here and will keep us here. Local tourism businesses also benefit. People on vacation usually seek out destinations that offer them the sense of being someplace, not just anyplace.

4. *Local businesses have a reduced environmental impact.* Locally owned businesses can make more local purchases requiring less transportation, and generally they set up shop in town or city centers as opposed to developing on the fringe. This generally means contributing less to sprawl, congestion, habitat loss, and pollution.

5. *Most new jobs are provided by local businesses.* Small local businesses are the largest employer nationally and, in our community, provide the most new jobs to residents.

6. *Customer service is better.* Local businesses often hire people with more specific product expertise for better customer service.

7. *Local business owners invest in the local community.* Local businesses are owned by people who live in the community, are less likely to leave, and are more invested in the community's future.

8. *Public benefits far outweigh public costs*. Local businesses in town centers require comparatively little infrastructure investment and make more efficient use of public services as compared with nationally owned chain stores.

9. *Competition and diversity lead to more choices*. A marketplace of tens of thousands of small businesses is the best way to ensure innovation and low prices over the long term. A multitude of small businesses, each selecting products based, not on a national sales plan, but on their own interests and the needs of their local customers, guarantees a much broader range of product choices.

10. *Supporting local enterprise encourages local investment*. A growing body of economic research shows that in an increasingly homogenized world, entrepreneurs and skilled workers are more likely to invest and settle in communities that preserve their one-of-a-kind businesses and distinctive character.

Adapted from the website of the Bellingham, Washington, chapter of Business Alliance for Local Living Economies (BALLE): sconnect.org.

Getting More Bang for Your Investment Buck

TRACY FERNANDEZ RYSAVY

Tracy Fernandez Rysavy is publications editor at Co-op America, coproducer of the Green Festival. Prior to joining Co-op America, she worked on the editorial staff at YES! magazine and taught English in an underresourced school in Louisiana through the Teach for America program.

Someone once asked us what she could do to increase the social impact of her socially responsible investments. She wanted to put her money where it would do the most good. The answer then was the same as it is now—community investments. And today, it's easier than ever to get the most social bang for your buck by investing in a very special vehicle—a community-developed pooled fund.

Community investing directs investor money into rebuilding low-income areas underserved by traditional financial services. In the United States and around the world, community investing institutions (CIIs) provide loans and other financial services to individuals in need who may otherwise not be able to access them due to lack of credit or income. CIIs supply capital for small businesses and vital services such as child care. In addition, these institutions also often provide education, mentoring, and technical support to guarantee the success of their loans—and of the communities they serve.

In 2002, Co-op America and the Social Investment Forum first issued our 1% (or More) in Community challenge, asking all our members to put 1 percent or more of our savings and investments into community investments. Together, our members are channeling over $500 million a year into community investments. Let's do even more this year and beyond.

A first step for many in meeting this challenge is to open an account in a community development bank or credit union. (For more information about these institutions, visit coopamerica .org/socialinvesting/communityinvesting.) If you'd like to go beyond checking accounts and certificates of deposit, consider a community development pooled fund. By investing in these funds, you can support a variety of CIIs with one investment, allowing you to spread your money around to advance issues and rebuild geographic areas that resonate with you.

Pooled Funds Defined

To understand community development pooled funds, you first have to understand what a community development loan fund (CDLF) is. A CDLF provides low-cost financing and development services to businesses, organizations, and individuals in low-income communities in the United States and around the world. The loans these funds make may help build affordable housing in California, create day care centers in North Carolina, or grant a microloan to help a poor woman in Guatemala set up her own business.

In short, the loans that CDLFs make vary, but they all use investor money to rebuild communities that need it most. Generally, CDLFs focus on one geographic or issue area. What makes them high impact is that investor money is tied up for a longer time than when one opens an account with a community investment bank or credit union. Also, many of these funds are able to reach the "highest-risk" borrowers who are most in need of capital to build their communities.

Pooled funds serve much the same function as CDLFs, except that instead of supporting one community or institution, these funds act as umbrella funds, where you invest in one fund, and your money is spread around to a variety of community investment institutions and loan funds. For example, one investment in the Calvert Foundation's pooled fund can allow you to support a community development organization that finances homeless shelters in Boston, another that provides microloans for impoverished women in India to start small businesses, and still another that gives opportunities to disadvantaged youth in San Francisco, all with one $1,000 investment.

Individuals of all income levels can invest in a pooled community investment fund, as can institutional investors such as faith-based organizations, businesses, and foundations (these qualify as program-related investments for private foundations). Different funds have different minimum investment amounts, ranging from $1,000 to $100,000 invested from 1 to 10 years.

Most pooled funds offer returns at market or below-market interest rates, which can be anywhere from 0 to 4 percent. These funds may offer you the opportunity to select your own interest rate and length of investment, with the knowledge that the lower you go and the longer you invest, the more social impact your investment will have.

Although pooled portfolio funds are not insured, their biggest benefit is that they allow you to diversify your community investments. In other words, instead of putting all of your community investment money into one fund and counting on it to survive and earn money, you divide your money among several funds to lessen the risk. The institutions that manage pooled funds generally back the entire portfolio up with a reserve of capital to insure against investor loss. All funds in this article have never lost a penny of investor funds.

Available Funds

One of the easiest community development pooled funds available to individuals is the Calvert Foundation's Community Investment Note.

When you invest in a Calvert Community Investment Note, your money supports a variety of community development organizations working in the affordable housing, small business, microcredit, and community development sectors. For a minimum investment of $1,000, you can choose to direct your Calvert Note investment to international organizations or to one of eight U.S. regions. You may also choose an interest rate of 0 to 2 percent for a 1- or 3-year note, or 0 to 3 percent for a 5-, 7-, or 10-year note.

For people with larger amounts of investment capital ($50,000 or more), Calvert offers the opportunity to create a Custom Note, where you may more closely align your investments with your values by choosing specific organizations, geographic areas, and social issues in which to invest.

In addition, Calvert has teamed up with several organizations to offer targeted pooled investment notes, including these:

- *The Jubilee Investing Initiative*—allows faith-based investors to place critical investment capital with microcredit and community development nonprofit lenders from Honduras to Zimbabwe
- *LGBT Community Investments*—supports lenders that provide important community facilities and services for the lesbian/gay/bisexual/transgender community
- *Gulf Coast Recovery Initiative*—Calvert's special pooled fund targets communities in the U.S. Gulf Coast and other affected regions that have been devastated by Hurricane Katrina. Your capital will be used to fund CIIs working to build affordable homes, finance community facilities, and support critical recovery and redevelopment.

RSF Social Finance offers its RSF Social Investment Fund for investors, which not only makes loans to CIIs, such as Ecologic Finance, but also grants loans directly to nonprofits and social enterprises across the country. The fund focuses on areas as diverse as children and education, environment and science, sustainable agriculture, arts and culture, economic and social renewal, disadvantaged communities, medicine and healing, and spiritual renewal.

"In addition to rebuilding low-income communities, RSF's program values the benefit of sustainable approaches to cultural issues such as healthy food systems and independent media to all populations," says RSF's Marta Becker.

When you loan money to RSF, RSF chooses how and where to distribute it among CIIs and organizations such as the Fellowship Community, an intergenerational living community providing elder care in a rural organic farm setting, or Bioneers, which promotes biological and cultural diversity, traditional farming practices, and environmental restoration.

You can invest in the RSF Social Investment Fund for a minimum of $1,000 invested for at least three months. Interest rates are variable, adjusted quarterly; the current rate at the time of publication was 3.83 percent.

Finally, Opportunity Finance Network (OFN) provides investors with the ability to support a nationwide network of community investment institutions (CIIs) through its Financing Fund. OFN is a national membership organization of CIIs that provide capital, technical assistance, and development services to support the revitalization of economically disadvantaged urban, rural, and reservation-based U.S. communities.

The OFN Financing Fund is open to institutions or individuals with a minimum of $100,000 to invest for at least seven years. Interest rates range from 0 to 4 percent and depend on the term and structure of your investment.

Taking the Plunge

You don't need a financial planner to invest in a pooled community investment fund, though you may choose to use one who can help you decide if this is the right type of investment for you. If you cannot afford the minimum investment but would like to support community investing, you can donate an amount of your choice to a community investment institution. Most gratefully accept donations in any amount, and your donation may be tax-deductible.

Please ask for a prospectus before investing in any community investment pooled portfolio, and consult with your financial adviser, if you have one. For more information about community investing at home or abroad, call Co-op America at (800) 58-GREEN, and ask for our free guide to Investing in

Communities, or purchase our new guide to international community investing for $6.

Over the past four years, members who have joined Co-op America's 1% (or More) in Community efforts have channeled over $1 billion into rebuilding areas most in need. A pooled portfolio is a great place for you to get involved.

Resources

- Calvert Foundation: (800) 248-0337, calvertfoundation.org
- Co-op America: coopamerica.org/go/communityinvest
- Opportunity Finance Network: (215) 923-4754, opportunity finance.net
- RSF Social Finance: (415) 561-3900

Climate Solutions at the Speed and Scale Necessary

ALISA GRAVITZ

Alisa Gravitz is executive director of Co-op America and executive coproducer of the Green Festivals.

The verdict is in: Our world is in the midst of a global climate crisis.

But before you feel overwhelmed, read on for a powerful, practical, cost-effective plan for how we can move forward to curb the climate crisis, without new nuclear and coal. It's a plan that uses technologies that are already proven, available, and in use today. And most important, it outlines the role you can play in what is perhaps the most important battle over the next 10 years.

If you've ever fallen in love, started a new job, or become a parent, then you've already done the most difficult things in life. Addressing the climate crisis is much easier and more straightforward!

And, as we bring forward climate solutions, we'll usher in a bright future—one that brings real energy security, more jobs, a cleaner environment, real progress on the war against poverty, and a safer, more joyful world.

The facts of the climate crisis are sobering indeed. Based on how fast greenhouse gases, particularly carbon dioxide, are accumulating in the atmosphere, the scientific consensus is that we have to move with lightening speed. Society's window is the next 10 years. We need to lay the groundwork immediately for decreasing carbon emissions while the global economy grows. The global scientific consensus is that by midcentury, we need to cut carbon emissions by 80 to 90 percent, and by the end of the century, we need to decrease annual carbon emissions to zero.

If we don't take actions, we'll more than double carbon emissions over the next 50 years. With business as usual, every one of the horrors chronicled in Al Gore's book and movie *An Inconvenient Truth* will come to pass. As Gore says, "If we don't get this one right, little else matters."

We have to move at a scale that is astounding—across all sectors of the economy from transportation to buildings to agriculture. We need to rapidly scale up all forms of energy efficiency and safe, renewable, noncarbon energy.

Here is a plan of action and time line that can match the size of the problem. It's a plan that our climate change team at Co-op America built, based on the work of scientists at Princeton University's Carbon Mitigation Initiative.

The Princeton team proposes stabilizing carbon emissions by dividing the task into seven "wedges" of equal size—each with the capacity to reduce carbon emissions by one billion tons per year by 2050.

It's time to take action. We have to achieve each wedge of carbon savings by 2050, with the next 10 years as the major ramp-up. It's like saving for retirement—if you start in your 20s, you can sail into retirement. If you wait until your early 60s, it's nearly impossible.

The scientists at Princeton list 15 ways of getting there in time. Out of the 15 ways they suggest, we need to achieve just 7 to hit the target. Every single suggestion on their list is based on current technology and know-how—already proven and already on the shelf.

At Co-op America, we really liked Princeton's building block approach, and we added our own filters to it. We screened out measures that are too dangerous, too costly, and too slow—like nuclear power, coal, and synfuels—and we beefed up those that are safe and cost-effective.

With these filters, we developed a plan that uses current technologies; is safe, clean, cost-effective; and is more than big enough to meet the climate challenge—12 steps when we only need 7.

Here is Co-op America's 12-step plan—to move our dependence away from fossil fuels and nuclear toward an energy future that is the foundation for a just and sustainable society.

Step 1: Increase Fuel Economy

Increase the fuel economy for 2 billion cars from an average of 30 miles per gallon to 60 miles per gallon by 2054.

For each of us personally, that means having a car that gets at least 40 miles per gallon by 2015, 55 by 2030, and 60 by 2050.

But note that the *global* fleet has to reach these averages, so each of us who can be better than average needs to do so right away to balance off each person who is less than average.

We also have to get Congress to change the fuel efficiency standards. Today they stand at 27.5, inching up to 35 by 2020—clearly nowhere near good enough.

The good news is that we have cars already on the market that can help us achieve this goal. Hybrids like the Prius and Insight and diesel vehicles run on waste-based veggie oil are helping thousands of families save on costs to their pocketbooks and our environment.

Step 2: Cut Back on Driving

Decrease car travel for 2 billion 30-mpg cars from 10,000 to 5,000 miles per year by 2050, through increased use of mass transit, telecommuting, and urban design that is conducive for walking and biking.

Here is a great trade-off: If your vehicle isn't meeting the mpg targets, cut back on driving. Ride your bike for short trips or errands—you'll be helping the climate and your health!

Step 3. Develop Zero-Emissions Vehicles

Plug-in hybrids and electric vehicles are the most efficient, cost-effective solution. They are best if powered by solar and wind. But even without renewable power, electric motors are much more efficient than the internal combustion engine. This means that electric vehicles powered through a coal-fired plant put 30 percent fewer carbon emissions into the atmosphere than gasoline-powered vehicles. Electric vehicles charged with the current grid mix produce 42 percent fewer emissions. It gets even better: according to the National Renewable Energy Lab, the United States could power 73 percent of our cars and light-duty trucks without building a single new power plant, if we charge the vehicles at night.

What about hydrogen fuel cells, you might ask? It's important to understand that hydrogen is *not* an energy source. It takes energy to make hydrogen. If you make it with solar or wind, then it is a renewable transportation fuel. If you make it with coal, our transportation system will do more to fuel the climate crisis than it does today. Plus, developing a hydrogen infrastructure—hydrogen stations instead of gas stations—is very expensive and energy-intensive.

Step 4: Biofuels

Develop biomass only as a short-term replacement for fossil fuel until better carbon-free technologies are developed, but only if biofuels are made from waste and can be made without displacing farmland and rainforests.

Biofuels from crops like corn are at best a tiny net carbon emission gain, at worst a loss—by the time you fertilize all the fields with petrochemicals, and fuel all the tractors and ethanol plants. When you calculate in the carbon cost of replacing farmland and forests, biofuels from crops are an enormous negative carbon loss. And, as we've already seen, making fuel from crops is a dangerous policy that forces prices up and people around the world to go hungry.

Step 5: Building Efficiency

Increase building efficiency by a fourth in all buildings and appliances—worldwide projected through 2050. Move to zero emissions for new buildings to achieve a 25 percent average reduction across all buildings.

To get these global averages, those of us in industrialized countries need to improve the efficiency of our homes by 50 percent in the next five years—only 10 percent a year. We can do this. After an avalanche cut off the power supply to Juneau,

Alaska, in the spring of 2008, the entire city—homes, businesses, schools, government buildings—achieved a 30 percent electricity reduction in just two weeks in order to avoid running expensive, dirty backup generators. Everyone can take simple, cost-effective measures to reduce their energy use by 10 percent a year.

Every time you replace an appliance, make sure it is at least 25 percent more efficient than the last one, and then recycle the old one—don't donate it so that it stays in service. If you build a new home or add on to your existing home, zero emissions is your goal

Step 6: Forests

Decrease tropical deforestation to zero, and double the rate of new tree plantings.

Keep on doing all your good work to recycle. It matters!

Step 7: Agriculture

Stop soil erosion. Apply "conservation tillage" techniques to cropland at 10 times the current usage. Encourage local, organic agriculture.

The food on our dinner plate travels an average of 1,500 to 2,500 miles from field to plate. We've got to get the average food miles down to no more than 200 to 500. That means going local.

We can also help by eating lower on the food chain. Choosing a vegetarian diet is about equivalent to choosing not to drive when it comes to climate change. Even if a vegetarian diet isn't for you, more meatless meals make a difference for the climate (and your health, too!).

Step 8: Ramp Up Wind Power

Add 3 million 1-megawatt windmills, 75 times the current capacity.

Step 9: Advance Solar Power

Add 3,000 gigawatt-peak solar photovoltaics, 1,000 times current capacity.

Not only are wind and solar cost-effective, but they are also great for providing peak power and baseload power, with the grid acting as a battery.

For utilities today, wind is a cost-effective option. In the past several years, wind installations have been the largest source of new utility-scale installations worldwide.

Many wind turbines are going up on farms and on Native American lands in the Midwest, generating clean energy and revenue to keep families on their farms and for sustainability projects in Indian country. What a great win-win for the environment and justice.

Right now, a group of experts, investors, and advocates is doing the same for solar. Co-op America's team is part of this leadership, and within three to five years, solar will be cost-competitive with coal.

This is a big win not only for climate change but also for the global war on poverty. Economic development experts say that a family's first 100 watts is their first step out of poverty—it's what a family needs to purify its water and get fuel for cooking without having to spend five hours a day gathering wood. That means kids can go to school and families can grow more food. Globally affordable solar will be this first step out of poverty for the two billion people around the world with no electricity.

Step 10: No New Coal

In addition to increasing wind and solar to make electricity, we have to decrease the use of coal. Starting today, no new coal plants; for any new plants built, an equal number of inefficient plants should be shut down.

The efficiency of all existing coal plants has to be increased from an average of 32 percent efficiency to 60 percent. And we have to shut down plants that don't meet this standard.

Step 11: Replace 1,400 Gigawatts of Coal with Natural Gas

This is a short-term step until zero-emissions renewable technologies can replace natural gas.

Step 12: Sequester CO_2 at Existing Coal Plants

Sequestration involves storing carbon dioxide underground, an unproven technology that may, nonetheless, be better than nothing.

What You Can Do

Now that you have the information on the big steps we need to take, here is the big ask: go to zero. Commit to getting to zero carbon emissions in every aspect of your life.

Here are five simple steps to get you there:

1. Find out what your carbon footprint is from your home, car, and air travel. Google "carbon footprint," and use any one of the great calculators to figure out your footprint.

2. Reduce your energy use as much as you can, and then buy carbon offsets for the rest. Carbon offsets take an amount of carbon out of the atmosphere equal to what you've put in. Trusted companies like Native Energy can do this for you. Repeat each year until you are at net zero energy—reduce, offset, repeat.

3. Get your workplace, your school, and your faith congregation to do the same.

4. Get your representative and senators to pass energy legislation that follow this 12-step plan on a national level.

5. Join with Co-op America to pressure the largest climate polluters—from Exxon Mobil to General Motors to the utility companies—to get going on their plans to follow these simple steps and at a scale large enough and fast enough to solve the problem. Take part in our actions by visiting our climate solutions website: climateaction.org.

The good news is we can do this. We have the technologies and the know-how. And the best news is that taking this action opens the door to more jobs, energy security, real progress on the war against poverty, a cleaner environment, and a safer world.

Green Pricing versus Green Citizenship

Green pricing programs, in which customers are asked to voluntarily pay a premium for varying amounts of electricity generated by renewable fuels, are sweeping the country. Green pricing programs encourage environmentally sensitive people to put their money where their mouth is. They encourage electricity marketers to develop national educational campaigns that promote clean energy. The largest single reason for residential customers to purchase electricity from an independent supplier is to buy green energy. In California, 90 percent of households that have switched suppliers have voted for green power with their electricity dollars. Companies like Patagonia and Toyota and cities like Santa Monica have voted to purchase electricity that is partially or fully generated by renewable energy.

While welcome, green pricing has serious limitations. Green pricing programs impose a stiff premium on consumers who want to be responsible and, in the aggregate, generate a relatively small amount of new renewable energy projects. In some cases, consumers are buying power from existing renewable energy facilities. Supporters of green pricing say that this is a short-term effect until the current capacity is soaked up. Others argue it will take a long time before that point is reached.

According to the Department of Energy's Green Power Network, the highest participation rate for a green pricing program thus far is the Capture the Wind program of Moorhead Public Service (MPS) in Minnesota. The program of MPS, a municipal utility, has been so successful that the utility plans on building a second wind turbine in order to satisfy requests from its customer-owners to enroll in the renewable energy program. More than 7 percent of the utility's 12,500 customers pay a premium of 0.5 cents per kilowatt-hour to get up to a third of their electricity from wind power. (see mpsutility.com for more info).

Green pricing requires a few customers to pay a substantial premium for relatively little power. A much better way for consumers to increase the supply of renewable energy is to exercise "green citizenship." If a significant majority of the customers of a given utility vote for green energy, the utility can purchase a larger amount of renewables and spread the costs over its entire customer base. Often 10 times the amount of green electricity can be purchased at a fraction of the cost for an individual household. To date, only one utility of which we are aware, the customer-owned Salem Electric Cooperative in Oregon, has adopted this strategy.

Customer-owned utilities (COUs), like the Salem Electric Cooperative, are more likely to enact green citizenship programs because they tend to be more responsive to the preferences of their customers. But where there is utility inaction, or where the electricity landscape is dominated by private monopolies, states can enact policies that embrace green citizenship and remove the onus of supporting renewables from the individual ratepayer to the collective base of all ratepayers.

Redefining Leadership

Hunter Lovins is the founder and president of Natural Capital Solutions, a nonprofit organization educating senior decision makers in business, government, and civil society to restore and enhance the natural and human capital while increasing prosperity and quality of life.

L et's start with some simple facts. Business as usual will not long endure. The financial markets are melting down. Real estate markets are losing value. Unemployment is rising. Our infrastructure is crumbling. We're losing every major ecosystem on the planet. The UN Millennium Ecosystem Assessment—a study by the world's leading scientists—concluded that we have polluted or overexploited two-thirds of the ecosystems on which human life depends, to the point that the ability of these ecosystems to sustain future generations can no longer be assumed.

This means that we have an unprecedented opportunity to reinvent companies, governments, and civil society and how we do business.

What we're losing are not just pretty vistas. These intact ecosystems give our economy about $35 trillion of services. These aren't on anybody's balance sheet, so we treat them as if they have a value of zero, but that's clearly daft. We don't know how to build an ecosystem. The folks at Biosphere 2 spent $200 million and couldn't keep eight people in clear air for two years. Maybe we should take care of the ecosystem we've got.

Something like 98 percent of the world's scientists say that climate change is real, and we are not going to like the consequences. Let's assume that the 2 percent who are skeptical are correct. If all you care about is maximizing your profit, you would do exactly what you would do if you were scared to death about climate change, because we can protect the climate at a profit. Companies are doing it. Dupont recently announced it was going to cut its emissions of greenhouse gases 65 percent below its 1990 levels, by 2010. During that time, Dupont reckons to get 10 percent of its energy from renewables. Dupont did this in the name of increasing shareholder value. It's kept energy use the same yet increased production 30 percent. It's hit its target globally and saved $3 billion.

Some insurance companies are now saying to companies, "If you don't take your carbon footprint seriously as a company, maybe we don't want to insure you, your officers, and directors." Imagine a business without officers' and directors' insurance.

JPMorgan Chase, with assets of $1.6 trillion and operations in more than 60 countries, is indexing bond issuances based on a company's carbon footprint. Citigroup, Deutsche Bank, JPMorgan Chase, UBS, and ABN Amro have committed $1 billion to finance the energy savings measures in municipal buildings in major cities around the world. In 2006, Goldman Sachs, the first Wall Street bank to issue an environmental policy, put $1 billion into clean-energy investments. It has also pledged to purchase more products locally. Credit Suisse followed by forming a renewable energy banking group that has done more than 40 deals, including the first capital markets financings in the biofuel and wind and solar power industries.

Since 2002, the British nonprofit, the Carbon Disclosure Project (CDP), has surveyed the *Financial Times* 500, the largest companies in the world, asking them to reveal their respective carbon footprints. Initially, only a few of the recipient corporations bothered to answer. In 2005, 60 percent answered. In 2006, 70 percent participated; and in 2007, 77 percent answered the survey.

Why the change? In the United States, the Sarbanes-Oxley Act makes it a criminal offense for a company's management to fail to disclose information, including such environmental liabilities as greenhouse gas emissions that could alter a reasonable investor's view of the organization. Perhaps more significantly, the CDP represents institutional investors with assets of over $31 trillion, up more than $10 trillion since 2006 and now constituting almost a third of all assets held by global institutional investors.

When General Electric announced Ecomagination, environmentalists claimed "greenwashing." And they were right. GE had just rebranded already-made products as green. Less than a year later, they noticed that those green-branded products had doubled in sales, whereas the rest of the company had only gone up 20 percent. The CEO of General Electric, Jeffrey Immelt, who once said the only green bone in his body was the one on the golf course, has now found that his green bone is attached to his wallet.

Over 800 mayors around the country have signed the U.S. Mayors' Climate Protection Agreement, pledging to abide by the Kyoto protocol, cutting their carbon emissions 7 percent below their 1990 levels. The mayor of Turtle River, Minnesota, said no city is too small. In Mount Vernon, New York, the mayor said the consequences of not acting are enormous. Salt Lake City, Utah, set carbon reduction goals of over 30 percent and met them.

My organization, Natural Capitalism, Inc. (natcapsolutions .org), wrote a manual that you can download for free. We are about to release a web-based tool for small businesses. These documents explain how to implement a profitable climate protection program in your community.

Berkeley, California, put in LED lights. It figured it'd save about $56,000 annually; it actually saved almost $90,000 a year. Scottsdale, Arizona, went with LEED (Leadership in Energy and Environmental Design) Gold building standards. The San Francisco Department of the Environment has a webpage devoted to climate protection, and it developed a comprehensive Environmental Plan for the city covering seven major areas of environmental restoration. Little Ratner Township, Pennsylvania, bought wind energy as a city. Flowermound, Texas, started a green building training program. In Ferndale, Michigan, if you drive a hybrid vehicle, you park for free.

Add up all the opportunities, and this country can save $300 billion a year. And we've done it before. After the 1979 oil price increase, we cut down energy use 15 percent while we grew our economy 16 percent, just through more efficient vehicle standards.

A typical community now is bleeding money, spending more than 20 percent of its gross income buying energy from outside. In 1979, Wes Birdsall, general manager of the Osage, Iowa, Municipal Utility, helped his customers use less electricity. He helped them get the services that energy gives: comfort in a building, cold beer, hot showers, and industrial power, while using less energy. His efficiency program saved this small rural town a million dollars a year, cut energy bills to half the state average, and unemployment to half the national average. With lower energy costs, more factories came to town. This genuine economic development is something that any town in the country can and should be doing. As our economy slides toward collapse, the green economy could become a survival strategy for communities and companies.

Policy tools can implement energy efficiency even faster. The New England states have created a carbon cap-and-trade system. California is following suit. Idaho recently adopted a plan from California that gives the utilities a share of what they save customers by cutting bills through efficiency. When this was put in place in California, the utility company PG&E invested over $150 million in the first year to help customers cut their bills through efficiency. Over the next couple of years, it saved customers over $2 billion, while adding $50 million a year to the company's shareholders.

Two key places to go hunting for energy savings are buildings and cars. Buildings use a third of our total energy, about two-thirds of our electricity. They're responsible for one-third to one-half of our greenhouse gas emissions and a lot of other waste. We know how to take any existing building and make it 3 or 4 times more efficient and new ones 10 times as efficient. Just improving indoor air quality through good green measures has an enormous economic return. Cutting lost sick time from sick building syndrome could add $58 billion to our economy. The increased worker productivity (6 to 16 percent verified increases) that comes with good green buildings would add another $200 billion. Good green features, like day lighting in schools, have resulted in higher test scores of 20 to 26 percent. Wal-Mart found that day lighting resulted in 40 percent higher sales.

Ideally, you combine efficiency with renewable energy. In Sacramento, California, the people voted to shut down Rancho Seco, the nuclear power plant, because it didn't work very well. The utility lost 1,000 megawatts all at once, but rather than invest in a coal plant or a gas plant, it invested first in efficiency, in renewable energy, and in massive tree planting to keep the city cooler and reduce the need for air conditioning. Now, more than 15 years later, the numbers are in. If it had continued running the nuclear power plant, electricity costs were projected to go up 80 percent. Instead, it held rates level for over a decade. This has kept 2,000 jobs and companies in place that threatened to leave if the rates went up. It generated 880 new jobs and enabled the utility company to pay off its debt. Any community can do this.

We're using oil at an increasing rate. Ninety percent of the oil we've ever consumed has been since about 1960, 50 percent of it since 1984. Our dependence on oil has enormous costs. The U.S. uses 25 percent of the world's oil right now, yet we own 3 percent of it. We import 60 percent of it, about a third of that, from a very unstable region.

Almost all of our oil goes to the transportation sector: cars, light trucks, 18-wheelers. We know how to build vehicles that are dramatically more fuel-efficient. We know how to deliver liquid fuel in more sustainable ways. I was on the podium with Richard Branson when he said that for the next 10 years he was planning to put Virgin Group profits into noncarbon fuel. When the media asked, "Why?" Branson said, "Look, I run an airline—I'm going to need fuel." And I said, "And he's going to make a boatload of money!"

We can also make fuel from farming and forestry wastes. It is very important that we do that right way. Agriculture now is profoundly unsustainable. If we load a liquid fuels program on top of unsustainable agriculture, we will create a massive disaster. Jane Goodall was right when she said that the way they are doing biodiesel in places like Malaysia—tearing out diverse forests to replace them with palm oil monocrops for export to the rich countries—is all wrong. The unsustainable way we're growing corn in the United States contributed to food riots on three continents. Again, though, we have answers. The Iowa State University bioeconomy program has shown that we can sustainably source biofuel feedstocks from polycultures of perennials and then use the fuel in very efficient vehicles. Even better, we can build the sorts of communities in which you can walk to where you need to go. We can invest in low-tech bicycles and high-speed trains.

We can choose a world based on renewable energy, and it will give us communities that are more livable communities. Wind energy capacity in the United States increased more than 25 percent in both 2006 and 2007. The fastest-growing form of energy supply is from photovoltaic solar cells. In California, Alameda County commissioned a 2.3-megawatt power plant on roofs. The utility paid for half, and it will save the county $700,000 a year. Some people are now calling for 25 percent renewable energy in the United States by 2025. But in Denmark, they will be using 60 percent renewable energy by 2010.

More and more people are realizing that business as usual is going to change. Happily we have some help. Janine Benyus wrote *Biomimicry: Innovation Inspired by Nature*, which points out that nature makes a wide array of products and services very differently than we do. Nature runs on sunlight. It doesn't make persistent toxins like nuclear wastes that hang around for hundreds of thousands of years. Nature shops locally.

For example, the abalone sits off the Pacific coast in seawater and makes an inner lining right next to the creature's body that's stronger than the best ceramics that we know how to make with very high-temperature kilns. The scientists at Sandia National Laboratories realized that an abalone excretes a protein that creates an electrically charged framework onto which seawater deposits this very beautiful inner lining. So they took an electrically charged silicone substrate, dipped it in alternating baths of calcium carbonate and a polymer, which is what seashell is, and the stuff self-assembled at the molecular level just the way it does for the abalone. This is industry that's clean by design. Nature runs a very rigorous testing laboratory in which the manufacturer recalls products that don't work. That's a cautionary tale for a young species like ours.

Our best designers are using nature's wisdom. John Todd, who just won the inaugural Buckminster Fuller Award, built a sewage treatment plant in Burlington, Vermont, that looked like a greenhouse. It was. He selected organisms from nature to do what they do in nature: detoxify part of the waste stream. They put one of these in the lobby of the new environmental studies building at Oberlin College in Ohio.

Traditionally, business only cared about profit. From that standpoint, the people and the planet are seen as a drag on profit. But there is a very strong business case for the "triple bottom-line" approach introduced by John Elkington, which says you don't just focus on profit—you have to balance it with a focus on people and planet. Some people call it the three E's: economy, ecology, and equity.

What we now realize is that the way to achieve outstanding financial performance is to behave responsibly to people and planet. When you cut your costs, as Dupont has, you enhance your bottom line. When the insurance companies say they won't insure you if you have a big carbon footprint, they reduce their risk. If you want labor productivity, a good green building will get you 6 to 16 percent higher labor productivity. When British Petroleum rebranded itself as Beyond Petroleum and started cutting its carbon emissions, they said this saved them $750 million, but even if it had cost money, it would have been worth doing because it makes them the kind of company where the best talent wants to be employed. If you want to drive innovation, increase your market share, or differentiate your brand, you should set up a goal like carbon neutrality. Wal-Mart is now driving sustainability up its supply chain, telling its suppliers to take their carbon footprint seriously.

Wal-Mart was run out of Germany because of the social critics. Changing its practices may be the only way to protect its franchise to operate. Wal-Mart has made some fairly significant pledges: dramatically increasing its vehicle fleet efficiency, cutting its use of energy, and striving to become 100 percent powered by renewable energy. It pledged to become the world's largest organic retailer. It's rebranding itself as affordable sustainability, because it doesn't have a choice.

This is the sustainability imperative. Wal-Mart's stock value had fallen 30 percent over the last four years. We have brought this movement to a point where we can say to the world's largest company, "If you don't become sustainable, you won't be around."

The companies on the Dow Jones Sustainability Index are the leaders in environmental policy, social policy, good governance policy, and they have 25 percent higher stock value than their competitors. Innovest has shown that the environmental leaders in entire industry sectors outperform the environmental laggards. In July 2007, a report from Goldman Sachs found that companies that are leaders in environmental, social, and good governance policies are outperforming the MSCI world index of stocks by 25 percent since 2005. Seventy-two percent of the companies on the list outperformed industry peers. The Economist Intelligence Unit found that the worst-performing companies are the most likely to have no one in charge of sustainability.

The companies that get this right will be first to the future, the billionaires of tomorrow. The only way to have a dynamic industrial economy is to use biomimicry, green chemistry, resource productivity, and renewable energy. These are the underpinnings of a new energy economy, a low-carbon economy, a sustainable, locally based economy with a high quality of life and durable jobs.

We need a new form of leadership. I think of Tolkien's book, *The Lord of the Rings.* Two fun-loving, unassuming, scared little hobbits took on an awesome task. They didn't know where they were going, but in the end, all the kings, warriors, and wizards stood by as the little people saved the world. Real leadership is all about ordinary people exhibiting extraordinary courage.

Organize! Organize! Organize!

BILL McKIBBEN

Bill McKibben is the author of many books, the most recent of which is Deep Economy: The Wealth of Communities and the Durable Future. *He and his Step It Up colleagues have recently formed 350.org, a global grassroots effort to press for international action on climate change.*

I n the summer of 2006, I was close to despair about how little was going on with climate change. Hurricane Katrina had come through. Hurricane Gore had come through. But still, nothing in Washington was happening.

I called up friends in Vermont and said, "Let's walk up to Burlington, and we'll sit in on the steps of the Federal Building, and maybe we'll get arrested and there will be a little story in the paper, and at least we will have done something." And my friends, as clueless as I, said, "OK." One was smart enough to call the police and ask what would happen if we did this. The police said, "Nothing." So instead, we organized this sort of pilgrimage; we started e-mailing people saying, "Come with us on a walk." And three weeks later, we left. For five days, we walked, camped in fields, ran programs in churches in the evening. By the time we arrived in Burlington, there were 1,000 people marching, which is a lot of people for Vermont.

It was more than enough to get all our candidates for federal office to come to our final rally on the shores of Lake Champlain. They agreed to work to cut carbon emissions 80 percent by 2050. This was a very radical proposition and way beyond anything in Congress. They all signed on, both the progressive Democrats and the conservative Republicans running for Congress.

On that occasion, the system worked the way it was supposed to. The only depressing thing was to open the paper the next day and read a story that said, "This protest of one thousand people may have been the largest gathering about climate change yet in this country." It seemed impossible, but the more I thought about it, the more sense it made. We'd built the superstructure of this movement, with scientists, engineers, policy people and economists, but we didn't have the mass participation to give it force.

When I say "we" in this case, I mean, six 22-year-olds just graduating from Middlebury College, where I teach, and me. We had neither money nor an organization. All we had was our wits, our convictions, and e-mail. We had connections to great regional organizers around the country. We started a website in January called StepItUp2007.org, and we asked people to organize rallies for April 14 to demand this same 80 percent reduction.

Because we didn't have any resources or experience, our expectations were low. Our hope was that we would organize maybe 100 demonstrations around the country, which would have been about 100 more than there'd been before. Instead, the thing took off in a viral fashion all across America, because people were haunted by the idea of global warming but hadn't known quite what to do. We kept hearing from people who said, "I was screwing in the new lightbulb over the kitchen table, and even as I was doing it, I thought to myself, 'This isn't going to stop global warming. What else am I going to do?'"

There were 1,400 rallies in all 50 states. It was unbelievably exciting. It was created entirely by people, like me, who had very little idea of what we were doing.

When I wrote *The End of Nature* in 1989, global warming was a hypothesis. The idea that human beings were pouring too much carbon into the atmosphere by burning coal and gas seemed scientifically valid but emotionally doubtful. How could we have grown large enough to actually alter the climate around us? It was a far-fetched idea. So the scientists set to work. By 1995, after launching satellites and weather balloons and coring glaciers and refining the huge super computer models, scientists were able to say with a great deal of consensus that human beings were warming the planet and this would be a serious problem. Since 1995, it's been as though the planet itself has been peer-reviewing that research to see if it was correct. All 10 of the hottest years on record have happened since 1995.

We have raised the temperature of the planet one degree Fahrenheit. In the early 1980s, early 1990s we would have said that one degree would have been just about enough to take us to the threshold of the global warming era. We'd expect to be starting to see effects, and the biggest effects would still be a decade or two, or a degree, down the road. It turns out that science dramatically underestimated how finely balanced the planet is. One degree has been enough to set every physical system out of kilter. It's showing up every place we can measure, and in a much larger scale, at a much more rapid pace, than we'd have guessed 20 years ago. This means that we don't have as much time as we thought we did to deal with this situation.

Our greatest climatologist, James Hanson, who works at NASA, has run the biggest computer model of the climate for the longest time. He defied a gag order from the Bush administration two years ago and gave a speech at the American Geophysical Union, where he said, "We have 10 years in order to reverse the worldwide flow of carbon into the atmosphere." We have seven years now. Seven years to start burning less oil, coal and natural gas or else we will guarantee an eventual atmospheric concentration of carbon dioxide at 450 parts per million. That will call into question the most fundamental principles of the Earth, as we know it. The great ice sheets of west Antarctica and Greenland are no longer considered stable. It's a completely different world. If we don't begin to shift our energy economy away from fossil fuel, the human cost will be astronomical, and it will begin with the poorest and most marginalized people, who, incidentally, are the people who have done the least to bring about this situation.

So it is incumbent on the 4.5 percent of humans who live in the United States who contribute 25 percent of the world's CO_2 to very quickly do something about it.

The good news is that, compared with 20 years ago, the set of solutions is much clearer now. When environmentalists talked about solar and wind power 20 years ago, we did it with our fingers crossed. Not anymore. Around the world, wind power is now the fastest-growing source of energy generation. Japan and Germany have become the two most solar-powered nations on Earth, not because they are all that sunny but because they have taken the situation seriously and have begun to do something about it.

For seven or eight years now, we've all been able to drive cars that get superb or at least pretty good gas mileage. I've been driving a hybrid vehicle for eight years that feels like old technology now. I'm looking forward now to a plug-in hybrid. It's ridiculous that we're still allowing—indeed, encouraging—cars that get 15 miles to the gallon. It's no longer necessary, if it ever was. We've begun to understand the power of conservation to quickly and cheaply drop the rate at which we use energy. Our wasteful habits are almost our ally because they mean that the first 30 or 40 percent reductions in our energy use will come easily, almost for free.

Yet while the solutions are clearer, the politics have grown murkier. One of the odd things about global warming is that probably the strongest response to it, at least rhetorically, was in 1988 when the first President Bush was running for election. We were talking of what was then called the greenhouse effect. And George Herbert Walker Bush said, "If I'm elected, I'm going to fight the greenhouse effect with the White House effect." And it was a good line. Too bad he didn't mean it. The Clinton administration talked a good game, but carbon emissions rose 12 percent during their years in office. The Bush Junior administration is a complete disaster on this question. The president walked away from his campaign commitment to do something about CO_2 within three weeks of taking office. He threw overboard the Kyoto process, the major international attempt to address this problem.

We have to remind our political leaders that this is not like most political issues. Most of the time in our system we advance by compromise and increment. We don't have that luxury on this issue. It's not environmentalists versus conservatives; it's human beings against the laws of chemistry and physics. The scientists have told us we need dramatic cuts for the next 50 years until our economy is essentially decarbonized. If we don't, the laws of physics and chemistry tell us, we are cooked, literally.

If we're going to make progress on the scale necessary, it's going to come by building a real movement for change now. It's got to be a movement as strong, morally urgent, and willing to sacrifice, just as the civil rights movement was a generation ago.

It needs to be a broad movement. It has to be a movement that wants social justice as well as environmental justice around the world, not just here at home. It's going to take all our ingenuity and generosity. And that's why in Step It Up we're calling for 80 percent reduction of CO_2 emissions by 2050. We're also calling for an immediate moratorium on new coal-fired power plants because of the carbon emissions and the other horrors they produce.

The third demand is a really powerful green jobs campaign aimed at low-skilled workers who have been shut out of our economy so far. One of the good things about the work that we need to do—insulating homes, putting solar panels on them—is that you can't outsource it to other countries. It has to be done here, and it can't be done by clicking a mouse—it has to be done by swinging a hammer. And that's work that must be done soon.

Another thing this movement needs is a vision of what the world looks like once all this happens, because it's going to be a different world. Many things about it are going to be very good indeed.

Ask the question: What kind of world has cheap energy created? Cheap energy and the prosperity that it built have allowed Americans to become the first human beings who essentially had no need of their neighbors. If you have a credit card and an Internet connection, you don't need anybody around you for anything. And we've tended to view that as the American Dream. It seemed like a dream come true, but it has not made us happier or more secure.

The reason is that all those things have involved hyperindividualism. We have been severing ties with community, losing the connections that, as socially evolved primates, are crucial to our survival. The average American eats meals with friends, family, or neighbors half as often as we did in the 1950s. The average American has half as many close friends as we did 50 years ago. Those changes gave way to all the stuff we've acquired in the meantime.

A world that moves more slowly has a more localized view of the world, and that is a good thing. One example: Farmers' markets are now the fastest-growing part of the food economy in this country; sales are up 10 or 12 percent a year. That is such good news environmentally, because we use a lot less energy getting food grown close to home. It's also good news socially; we connect with the people who grow our food and get to learn about food production in a direct way that is not possible in the corporate-controlled food system.

A few years ago, a pair of sociologists followed shoppers around a supermarket and then followed them around a farmers' market. When they followed them around the farmers' market, the shoppers had 10 times more conversations per visit than at the supermarket. The heaviest users of farmers' markets are ethnic immigrant communities in big cities—people who are not as removed historically from traditional food systems.

That's tremendously good news. Conversations are the stepping-stones we need to make changes in every other area. They remind us of what it is that actually gives us pleasure and meaning to our lives.

Those Step It Up rallies were a model for that sort of community. We thought, "There's something wrong about telling people to travel across the country, spewing carbon behind them, to protest global warming. Let's do this closer to home." We thought that people would be able to take the genius of their particular place and use it in a way that they could explain to their neighbors what was happening.

All around the country people did amazing things. In Key West, Florida, we have the only coral reefs in the continental United States. Coral reefs are an ecosystem that will be gone in 30 or 40 years as the oceans keep warming. In Key West, lots of people in scuba gear went down off the coral reefs and held up big signs. Huge fish swam in and around this huge rally. It was so beautiful.

In Jacksonville, Florida, they chose the parking lot of the Jacksonville Jaguars football stadium as a sacred place. They had a big party and got a crane and lynched a yacht 20 feet up in the air, and they said, "That's where the ocean is going to be if Greenland melts."

I was in Lower Manhattan, and we all joined hands and made a sea of people to form a kind of human tide line to show where ocean levels will cover some of the most expensive real estate in the world if the sea rises just a few feet.

If we're going to get to do the beautiful long-term work of changing this world to one that works for everyone, then we also have to do the tough short-term political work of stopping this runaway train before it obliterates all chance of effective action. And that means just the kind of politics and the kind of movement that I've been describing.

Jobs 1, 2, and 3 are to organize, organize, organize. And if you have some energy left after that, put in a new lightbulb, and put in a new Congress.

Conclusion: Where Do We Go from Here?

Kevin Danaher and Alisa Gravitz

Thanks for taking this trip with us through the Green Festival and the green economy.

To pass on to our grandchildren healthy, thriving communities, instead of a desperate world, we need to accelerate the transition to the green economy: one that works for people and planet, social and economic justice, community and environmental health. So here are some ideas for future action to speed up the paradigm shift that can save humanity from itself.

First, we need to change the story. The green economy story is changing the culture of the progressive movement from one of protest—a narrative about "them," the people in power—to a narrative about us. How do we recruit more people to the triple-bottom-line economic model (integrating social and economic justice, environmental restoration, and financial sustainability) that is steadily replacing the outdated profit-maximizing economic model?

Our analogy is the *Titanic*. The corporate economic model that exploits nature and creates greater inequality has hit the iceberg of unsustainability, and it is sinking. So, we have two types of political activity to choose from. We can either run around the decks of the *Titanic* screaming "I protest—this boat sucks!" or we can get busy building a solar-powered, wind-powered boat with a party on deck, people with drinks (organic juice, beer, and wine, of course) in hand, dancing to cool music, and we pull up alongside the *Titanic*, and people will jump willingly onto our boat.

Doing it this positive way means we are not insulting people's intelligence by saying, "You must be stupid; you are on a sucky boat." We are just confidently offering them a more practical, joyful way of moving forward.

There are two kinds of analysis: the analysis of the way things *are*, and the analysis of the way we can *make things be*. So, whenever anybody starts spouting that cynical "We can't do it" line, we need to shift them over to the analysis of the activist.

We need to push capital into the triple-bottom-line type of investing—for people and the planet. We have to get away from the short-term perspective of the current investment system, which seeks to maximize profits on a quarterly, even daily and sometimes minute-by-minute basis. We have to move from this "short-termism," which is at the root of the problem with our current economic system, to one that takes the long-term view. The long view would be about not just sustainability but environmental restoration and making sure each person on the planet, and every community, has what they need to thrive.

The start of this way of thinking about investing is already here. More than $2 trillion is invested in socially screened investments. If you look at a pie chart of the different kinds of socially responsible investments (stocks, bonds, community investing), the category of community investing is the smallest piece, but it is the fastest growing.

We are now seeing a growing competition between a single-bottom-line economy that is all about money and a triple-bottom-line economy that balances social equity, environmental restoration, and financial sustainability. Our prediction is that the triple-bottom-line economy is the stronger model and will eventually prevail, but we need to accelerate that transition.

We are in the process of redefining free enterprise from "the freedom of big corporations" to go anywhere and do anything to people and planet, to "the freedom of everyone to be enterprising." The current system concentrates capital upward in the class structure; we want to push capital down and out. Jim Hightower says, "Capital is like cow manure. If you concentrate it in a big pile, it stinks. If you spread it out evenly, it makes things grow."

Indeed, the choices you make every day can accelerate the growth of the green economy. By living, buying, and investing green, you are nurturing the choices that sustain us all. Two out of three Americans now use some form of holistic health care. Organic food, Fair Trade–certified coffee, and green buildings now represent 2 to 5 percent of the food, specialty coffee, and building sectors. All sectors of the green economy are growing faster than their conventional counterparts.

With each green step you take, you help solve our planet's problems. When you buy Fair Trade, you ensure a fair wage for producers around the world. By choosing local, organic food, you reduce the dangerous pesticides used on conventional crops, prevent farmworkers from exposure to these toxins, and save family farms. By making your home more energy-efficient, you improve the comfort of your home and save money, curb climate change, and create green jobs. And the more energy we save, and the more renewables we bring online, the faster we'll be able to shut down dirty coal plants, breathe cleaner air—and stop the economic injustice of toxic facilities in communities of color.

We need to connect the dots, building even more bridges among people who care deeply about the future. We have social justice groups, environmental groups, save-the-dolphins groups, save-the-forest groups; and we have people working on inner-city poverty, homelessness, health care, spirituality, improving education, and many other issues. People are starting to understand that the problems are interconnected, and so are the solutions. We are learning to accelerate our bridge building among these issues, people, and groups, creating greater synergy. So we are seeing more low-income housing projects with solar energy on the roof, and organic farmers actively opposing wars for oil.

We need to network the green thinkers in the three main sectors of government, nonprofit, and private enterprise. What we show in a previous book, *Building the Green Economy: Success Stories from the Grassroots,* is that alliances of nonprofits, green companies, and government agencies can, together, change our society from the bottom up. This movement is creating a different political model. The old political model—of the Republicans, Democrats, Marxist-Leninists, and so on—was to create a political party that could somehow gain state power and then change the economy from the national government level downward. The green economy movement is reversing that entire process, saying, "Get control of the economy at the local level and build up from there, so when you eventually get control of government at higher levels, you have already changed the economy at the grassroots, and those changes are much more likely to last if they are rooted in local communities, under local control."

You can see the power of this growing everywhere. In San Francisco and other cities, the movement is passing laws that say, for example, "When the city government is buying stuff, it has to be shown that the stuff was not made in a sweatshop." People are coming together—from Cape Ann, Massachusetts; to Ashland, Oregon; to Chicago, Illinois; to Sarasota, Florida—they are coming together to build resilient communities. They are connecting the dots, helping create strong local food systems, helping everyone save energy, developing new green-collar jobs for youth and low-wage workers, involving music, art, and culture—in short, creating a world that works for all.

The Honeybee Economy

We have to design everything with a cradle-to-cradle perspective. Think of the honeybee. Does the honeybee hurt the flower when it makes honey, or does it help the flower when it makes honey? Nature operates on a totally closed loop. In nature, there is no waste. People say, "Throw it away." There is no "away."

Bill McDonough, the famous green architect, says, "Take the exhaust pipe of the car, bend it back into the cab of the car, and tell the engineers to make that OK." With that approach, we'd get really different cars: ones that are clean, safe, and fuel-efficient. We would give this idea a little political twist and say, "Take the smokestack of the factory, put it into the living room of the owner of the factory, and then tell the engineers to make that OK." And factories would clean up their acts, really fast.

We need to spread green measurement of growth. What is the ideology of the cancer cell? Grow, grow, grow. The cells of a metastasizing tumor have no concern for their impact on neighboring cells. What is suburban sprawl? What does the traditional capitalist property developer do? They don't care about their impact on the environment. It is grow, grow, grow: the ideology of the cancer cell.

We need to favor life values over money values. The world has two systems in conflict: the money cycle and the life cycle. Our species needs to answer this question: Should we have money values dominate the life cycle, or should life values rule over the money cycle?

Here is an analogy you should try out on people: the *Titanic* versus the party boat (the Green Festival boat). One is based on money values, and the other is based on life values. The money values model says, "If you have a 2,000-year-old redwood tree, it is not a gift of the Creator to be preserved for the enjoyment of future generations; it is $250,000 worth of lumber on the lumber market. Cut that sucker down."

A life values economy, on the other hand, has a different set of values that is sometimes summarized as biomimicry: observing how nature does things and imitating that process.

Mother Nature's beta (testing) phase has been billions of years. She has tested all these systems and weeded out the ones that didn't work. Mother Nature loves all of her children— regardless of size, species, number of legs, amount of fur, color of hair, race, or religion. We need to do the same.

What is the most universal human value that has survived thousands of years of history in many different cultures? It is "Do unto others as you would have others do unto you." Now the task before us is how do we take that word *others* and expand it to include all species. As William McDonough says, "How do we love all the children of all species for all time?"

We now know from neurological science, if I do an act of kindness toward someone, her serotonin levels go up, my serotonin levels go up, and for everyone who observe that act of kindness, their serotonin levels go up. Low serotonin is associated with anxiety, depression, schizophrenia, and suicide. When you are kind and considerate of others, you raise the levels of healthy chemicals in your body (DHEA, immunoglobulin B, serotonin, dopamine, adrenaline) and make other people feel good at the same time. We have the ability to heal our communities and heal the planet at the same time by being generous of spirit.

We have got to change the definition of love from the Hollywood version of two individuals creating an island of happiness in a sea of misery, to big love, the kind of love Jesus and Mahatma Gandhi and Martin Luther King Jr. were talking about: the love of all life, unconditional love, the automatic love a baby has for its parents.

The project before us is how to save humanity from itself. Yes, that sounds like a big project, but I. F. Stone used to say, "If you expect an answer to your question during your lifetime, you are not asking a big enough question." The masons who laid the foundation layer of cathedrals in Europe that took centuries to build knew that they would not see the final product of their work, but they knew they had to do very solid, precise work because of all the weight that was going to come on top of their work. That is the consciousness we need now. We are called on by history to lay the foundation for a future global economy with no starving children, no clear-cut forests, no endangered species, and no wars for oil.

We need to muster the courage to become good ancestors. We need to rediscover our spines and get up on our hind legs and struggle against the obstacles that we confront, so we can accelerate the transition to the green economy and not leave a burnt cinder of a planet for our great grandchildren.

We can do this. Let's get going! We hope this book gave you some new ideas and the motivation to accelerate your good works for *your* future, and ours, and for all life on this beautiful planet.

And we'll see you at the next Green Festival—to celebrate, learn, and pick up more inspiration for the road ahead.

Life is either a daring adventure, or nothing.

—HELEN KELLER

Resources

Green Building Resources

To help you navigate the many green options, here is a list of useful websites, with descriptions of what you can find on each.

greenfestivals.org: Green Festival's website provides a wealth of resources for taking action on social justice, ecological balance and economic sustainability. You will find: free streaming of audio and video of the Green Festival speakers and programs; a speakers directory linking you to diverse speakers and their books, podcasts and presentations; en exhibitors directory linking you to the best of the green economy, businesses that have passed Co-op America's strict screens for social and environmental responsibility; green economy news and information, and of course, the speakers and programs for upcoming Green Festivals. Use the website to contact us and propose speakers and other ideas for the Green Festivals, and connect to Global Exchange and Co-op America, the two organizations that bring you Green Festival. In 2009, our Green Festivals will be in Seattle, Denver, Chicago, Washington, DC, and San Francisco.

coopamerica.org: Co-op America's website provides you with the resources you need to green your life, green your business and green the world. Learn about everything from the best ways to save energy to how to invest in your community. The Green Pages section of this website links you to over 5,000 green businesses, screened and approved as authentically socially and environmentally responsible, and the Responsible Shopper section gives you the good, the bad and the ugly about the nation's biggest corporations and consumer brands. You can also take action on key green economy issues such as climate change—including campaigns to stop dirty energy and advance clean energy, fair trading solutions—including campaigns to stop sweatshops and advance Fair Trade, and stopping corporate irresponsibility.

globalexchange.org: Global Exchange has diverse programs: Reality Tours take people to more than 30 global destinations, mainly,in the global south; seven fair trade stores market the products of grassroots development groups in the global south as a way to help them generate revenue while educating people in the U.S. about positive development efforts around the world; their corporate accountability campaigns have forced companies such as Nike, the GAP, and Starbucks to change their policies to ensure more social justice and environmental restoration; the Green Alternatives Department works on the Green Festivals, Environmental Service Learning programs in San Francisco high schools, Green Careers programming with City College of San Francisco, and the Youth Unity Coalition for Action Now (YUCAN) in San Francisco.

buildinggreen.com: An independent publishing company out of Brattleboro, Vermont. This group brings its members accurate and up-to-date green design information and research through publications, case studies, a green products directory, and numerous other online tools.

builditgreen.org: A nonprofit membership organization based out of Berkeley that works to promote energy- and resource-efficient building practices within the state of California. This group works with stakeholder groups in the housing industry to encourage the adoption of green building practices. The website also offers a green products database as well as information on green building events, workshops, and GreenPoint Rating, a California-specific third party certification.

ecodesign.org: Founded by Sim Van der Ryn in 1969, the Ecological Design Institute (EDI) was one of the first established nonprofit organizations that works to apply a whole systems approach and the principles of ecodesign and sustainable living to research and education. Working with its local community through schools, organizations, and businesses, the EDI works to promote and support a more livable future through educational workshops.

energy.gov: The U.S. Department of Energy site includes sections for consumers, educators, students, and employees. Resources include energy-saving tips, improving energy efficiency in buildings and homes, and the Energy Star program. The "Learn More" section of each page has even more resources and links.

energystar.gov: This site is sponsored by the U.S. Environmental Protection Agency and the Department of Energy. There are descriptions of the Energy Star certification program, lists of certified products, and tips for heating and cooling efficiently. Also available: green building resources, studies about energy use, case studies, tips for developing a green building policy, and views of Energy Star–qualified new homes.

globalgreen.org: Information on this site includes green building cities and schools, climate change and energy, water, recycling, and a Green Building Resource Center. The section on green buildings and energy efficiency lists a wide array of resources and links.

greenmaven.com: A search engine that focuses on green-conscious websites offering an unending amount of information connecting you to the green world.

greenroundtable.org: This site is the home of the Green Roundtable, Inc. (GRT), an independent nonprofit organization based out of Boston whose mission is to mainstream green building and sustainable practices in hopes of becoming obsolete. Through policy advocacy, outreach education, informational events, and other strategies, this organization works with major building stakeholders to work toward a goal of making building green the standard.

greensource.construction.com: A collaboration program between separate companies who meet frequently to create and maintain this website and its complimentary magazine *Green Source*. Both offer information about green building practices, products, technology, news, case studies, and the latest in green resources. The art, editorial, and production staffs from BuildingGreen and the architects and engineers from McGraw-Hill Construction meet face-to-face regularly to bring their readers this award-winning magazine and website.

sustainablebusiness.com: This website provides up-to-date news and networking services from around the globe to help green companies grow. Supporting businesses from all sectors, including energy, organics, building, and investing, SustainableBusiness.com offers a breadth of information on green investing and stocks, green jobs, events, and other network connections.

thegreenguide.com: This is a magazine by National Geographic. You can pay for a subscription or read many of the articles online for free. There are articles about green products, green practices to adopt, green home improvements, health and the environment studies, and health risks posed by some products and practices. Archives of past editions are also available, including Spanish-language versions.

usgbc.org: The U.S. Green Building Council's website contains everything you need to know about Leadership in Energy and Environmental Design (LEED) certification. It includes a description of LEED certification processes, links to local chapters, conference updates, and resources. Some resources are members-only, but many LEED resources are accessible to everyone.

Consumer and Recycling Information

ase.org: This is the site for the Alliance to Save Energy. There is information for consumers, educators, policymakers, and energy professionals. Some features: program lists and descriptions, international energy use, topics (including buildings, insulation, lighting, and federal energy use), and quick facts and reports.

compostguide.com: An introduction to and operation guide to making your own compost.

coopamerica.org: Co-op America, an organization that works to harness economic power to promote change, runs this site. Includes National Green Pages, activism articles, fair trade guides, a resource section, and a hot topics section with articles and resources.

earth911.org: Earth 911 is a website with information about recycling, energy saving, household items, and other green/sustainable subjects. There are also current news articles that relate to the subject.

greenbiz.ca.gov: This is the site of the Bay Area Green Business Program. There are lists of products, services and organizations, local resources and partners, and members of the California Green Business Network. Also includes links to regional, state, and national resources and organizations, and industry-specific resources and professional associations. The Becoming Green page has useful tips and resources.

greencitizen.com: Green Citizen, an electronics recycling company, picks up old electronics from businesses and special drop-off sites. It recycles items on a per-item fee basis and provides a list of partner businesses. Under the "Learn More" tab, the Resource Center has relevant laws, useful websites, recommended readings, and kids' resources.

greenopia.com: Greenopia is an extensive directory of local (and national) ecofriendly listings within and around Los Angeles and San Francisco. With a one- to four-leaf rating system, you can browse this book (and website) to find only the most sustainable businesses, with sections ranging from Art & Leisure, Fashion & Beauty, Food & Drinks, to Party Planning, Eco Events, and Shopping Picks. This companion website also features forum discussions and other resources such as "How to Be Greener Guide" and "Ask the Greenopia Team."

greenseal.org: A nonprofit organization that uses science-based certification to transform the marketplace through the promotion of environmentally responsible products and services. Green Seal offers advice and assistance to manufacturers and consumers in order to help individuals and business make more informed decisions about the materials and operations we invest in.

sfenvironment.org: SF Environment is a department of the San Francisco city government that works to promote a healthier and more sustainable future for San Francisco through innovative and wide-ranging environmental programs.

stopwaste.org: A public agency operated by three Alameda County organizations: the Waste Management Authority, Source Reduction, and the Recycling Board. This website offers a host of materials related to recycling, composting, landscaping, and building as well as business, consumer, and local community resources.

thegreenoffice.com: A website dedicated to the search for post-consumer recycled office supplies and products. With the Co-op America Business Seal of Approval, Bay Area Green Business Program Certified, CERES Annual Sustainability Reporting, and Green House Gas Emissions Offsetting, this website reports on the greener choices for office supplies with a "Green Screen" labeling system that ranks the greenness of every product.

Calculating Your Ecological Footprint

climatecrisis.net: This is the website from *An Inconvenient Truth*. You can buy the DVD, view the science and facts cited in the movie, learn how to take action, join the virtual march, get energy-saving tips, and calculate your carbon footprint using a more detailed form.

epa.gov/climatechange/index.html: The U.S. Environmental Protection Agency hosts this site. There are resources about greenhouse gases, health and environmental effects, U.S. climate policies, clean energy, and the Energy Star program. You can also calculate your emissions.

myfootprint.org: This is a link from the Earth Day Network page (earthday.net). You can get a rough estimate of your ecological footprint.

Gardening/Landscaping

anniesannuals.com: Annie's Annuals and Perennials. A Bay Area nursery that grows plants naturally. You can browse by plant type or flower color, see an A–Z list of its plants, and order catalogs or by mail.

commongroundinpaloalto.org: The Common Ground Organic Garden Supply and Education Center is a project of Ecology Action, a nonprofit organization. The site includes classes and events, newsletters, articles, products, and resources (gardening tips, planting calendar, eating sustainably).

ecolandscaping.org: The website for the Ecological Landscaping Association. Includes events, publications, and resource links.

gardenfortheenvironment.org: Garden for the Environment's site (sponsored by the Haight Ashbury Neighborhood Council). Lists of classes offered, news and events, resources and contacts, and volunteer opportunities.

plantsf.org: Plant SF, a San Francisco–based organization, promotes permeable landscaping. The site has articles, news, resources and contacts, how-to guides, and explanations of permeable landscaping.

Water Conservation

cuwcc.org: Site by the California Urban Water Conservation Council. Includes news, new products, and technical resources.

sfwater.org: A site by the San Francisco Public Utilities Commission. View press and news, sustainability plans, water conservation tips, tools and reports, rebates, and resources for businesses or homes. A useful site.

Acknowledgments

All books are a team process, and this book is no exception. We would like to thank the hundreds of speakers who have presented at the seven years of Green Festivals across the country. Their talks are freely streamable in audio and video formats at greenfestivals.org.

Individuals we would like thank for their help in producing this book include Mary Ambrose, Tracy Fernandez Rysavy, Andrew Korfhage, Samantha Saarion, Lily Liang, Peter Richardson, Scott Jordan, Melissa Edeburn, and Monique Lusse.

And, of course, we send big hugs of gratitude to the large and growing team that produces the Green Festivals: Greg Roberts, Denise Hamler, Georgia Malki, Alan Van de Kamp, Karri Winn, Alix Davidson, Isabel Schechter, Jenny Heins, Zakiya Harris, Emily Adler, Alesha Reardon, Amanda Dufon, Amy Garcia, Annette Kamm, Vanessa Driscoll, Cindy Warlick, Cory West, Claire Hester, Dennis Donnelly, Geary Douglas, Glenn Geffcken, Janie Castaldo, Jennie Caissie, Jennifer Fuddy, Joseph Malki, Junko Yamamato, Ken Cousins, Kristen Kennedy, Lindsey Newkirk, Matt Walsh, Sage Linden, Sam Ruark,

Sherry Spurlin, Syd Fredrickson, Tavin Cole, Todd Hunsdorfer, Tomer Shapira, Al Parisi, Pandora Thomas, Michael Bootzin, Ashley Erickson, Chip Py, Dana Christianson, Jessica Long, Kathy Harget, Mo Alem, Prianjali Mascarenhas, Samantha Saarion, Shireen Karimi, Vickie Kreha, Yochi Zakai, Desiree Wolford, Jesse DiLaura, Frank Locantore, Courtney Baily, Kirsten Moller, Medea Benjamin, Natalie Mottley, Steve Ubiera, Paula Jenkins, Corina Nolet, Adrienne Fitch-Frankel, and the great teams at Ranch 7, EarthSite, and Organic Works.

About the Editors

Kevin Danaher is a cofounder of Global Exchange (global exchange.org), founder and executive coproducer of the Green Festivals (greenfestivals.org), and executive director of the Global Citizen Center (globalcitizencenter.org). Kevin received his PhD in sociology from the University of California at Santa Cruz. He is the coauthor, with Jason Mark and Shannon Biggs, of *Building the Green Economy: Success Stories from the Grassroots* (PoliPointPress, 2007).

Alisa Gravitz is executive director of Co-op America (coopamerica. org) and executive coproducer of the Green Festivals. For 25 years, she has led Co-op America, the national green economy organization. It develops marketplace solutions to social and environmental problems and operates the nation's largest green business and consumer network. Its publications include the *National Green Pages* and *Real Money*. Alisa earned her MBA from Harvard University.

OTHER BOOKS FROM POLIPOINTPRESS

The Blue Pages: A Directory of Companies Rated by Their Politics and Practices
Helps consumers match their buying decisions with their political values
by listing the political contributions and business practices of over 1,000
companies. $9.95, paperback.

Rose Aguilar, *Red Highways: A Liberal's Journey into the Heartland*
Challenges red state stereotypes to reveal new strategies for progressives.
$15.95, paperback.

Jeff Cohen, *Cable News Confidential: My Misadventures in Corporate
Media*
Offers a fast-paced romp through the three major cable news channels—
Fox CNN, and MSNBC—and delivers a serious message about their fail-
ure to cover the most urgent issues of the day. $14.95, paperback.

Marjorie Cohn, *Cowboy Republic: Six Ways the Bush Gang Has Defied
the Law*
Shows how the executive branch under President Bush has systematically
defied the law instead of enforcing it. $14.95, paperback.

Joe Conason, *The Raw Deal: How the Bush Republicans Plan to Destroy
Social Security and the Legacy of the New Deal*
Reveals the well-financed and determined effort to undo the Social Secu-
rity Act and other New Deal programs. $11.00, paperback.

Kevin Danaher, Shannon Biggs, and Jason Mark, *Building the Green
Economy: Success Stories from the Grassroots*
Shows how community groups, families, and individual citizens have protected their food and water, cleaned up their neighborhoods, and strength-
ened their local economies. $16.00, paperback.

Reese Erlich, *The Iran Agenda: The Real Story of U.S. Policy and the Middle East Crisis*
Explores the turbulent recent history between the two countries and how
it has led to a showdown over nuclear technology. $14.95, paperback.

Steven Hill, *10 Steps to Repair American Democracy*
Identifies the key problems with American democracy, especially election practices, and proposes ten specific reforms to reinvigorate it. $11.00, paperback.

Markos Kounalakis and Peter Laufer, *Hope Is a Tattered Flag: Voices of Reason and Change for the Post-Bush Era*
Gathers together the most listened-to politicos and pundits, activists and thinkers, to answer the question: what happens after Bush leaves office? $29.95, hardcover; $16.95 paperback.

Yvonne Latty, *In Conflict: Iraq War Veterans Speak Out on Duty, Loss, and the Fight to Stay Alive*
Features the unheard voices, extraordinary experiences, and personal photographs of a broad mix of Iraq War veterans, including Congressman Patrick Murphy, Tammy Duckworth, Kelly Daugherty, and Camilo Mejia. $24.00, hardcover.

Phillip Longman, *Best Care Anywhere: Why VA Health Care Is Better Than Yours*
Shows how the turnaround at the long-maligned VA hospitals provides a blueprint for salvaging America's expensive but troubled health care system. $14.95, paperback.

Marcia and Thomas Mitchell, *The Spy Who Tried to Stop a War: Katharine Gun and the Secret Plot to Sanction the Iraq Invasion*
Describes a covert operation to secure UN authorization for the Iraq war and the furor that erupted when a young British spy leaked it. $23.95, hardcover.

Susan Mulcahy, ed., *Why I'm a Democrat*
Explores the values and passions that make a diverse group of Americans proud to be Democrats. $14.95, paperback.

Christine Pelosi, *Campaign Boot Camp: Basic Training for Future Leaders*
Offers a seven-step guide for successful campaigns and causes at all levels of government. $15.95, paperback.

William Rivers Pitt, *House of Ill Repute: Reflections on War, Lies, and America's Ravaged Reputation*
Skewers the Bush Administration for its reckless invasions, warrantless wiretaps, lethally incompetent response to Hurricane Katrina, and other scandals and blunders. $16.00, paperback.

Sarah Posner, *God's Profits: Faith, Fraud, and the Republican Crusade for Values Voters*
Examines corrupt televangelists' ties to the Republican Party and unprecedented access to the Bush White House. $19.95, hardcover.

Nomi Prins, *Jacked: How "Conservatives" Are Picking Your Pocket — Whether You Voted for Them or Not*
Describes how the "conservative" agenda has affected your wallet, skewed national priorities, and diminished America—but not the American spirit. $12.00, paperback.

Cliff Schecter, *The Real McCain: Why Conservatives Don't Trust Him— And Why Independents Shouldn't*
Explores the gap between the public persona of John McCain and the reality of this would-be president. $14.95, hardcover.

Norman Solomon, *Made Love, Got War: Close Encounters with America's Warfare State*
Traces five decades of American militarism and the media's all-too-frequent failure to challenge it. $24.95, hardcover.

John Sperling et al., *The Great Divide: Retro vs. Metro America*
Explains how and why our nation is so bitterly divided into what the authors call Retro and Metro America. $19.95, paperback.

Daniel Weintraub, *Party of One: Arnold Schwarzenegger and the Rise of the Independent Voter*
Explains how Schwarzenegger found favor with independent voters, whose support has been critical to his success, and suggests that his bipartisan approach represents the future of American politics. $19.95, hardcover.

Curtis White, *The Spirit of Disobedience: Resisting the Charms of Fake Politics, Mindless Consumption, and the Culture of Total Work*
Debunks the notion that liberalism has no need for spirituality and describes a "middle way" through our red state/blue state political impasse. Includes three powerful interviews with John DeGraaf, James Howard Kunstler, and Michael Ableman. $24.00, hardcover.

For more information, please visit www.p3books.com.

ABOUT THIS BOOK

This book is printed on Cascade Enviro100 Print paper. It contains 100 percent post-consumer fiber and is certified EcoLogo, Processed Chlorine Free, and FSC Recycled. For each ton used instead of virgin paper, we:

Save the equivalent of 17 trees
Reduce air emissions by 2,098 pounds
Reduce solid waste by 1,081 pounds
Reduce the water used by 10,196 gallons
Reduce suspended particles in the water by 6.9 pounds.

This paper is manufactured using biogas energy, reducing natural gas consumption by 2,748 cubic feet per ton of paper produced.

The book's printer, Malloy Incorporated, works with paper mills that are environmentally responsible, that do not source fiber from endangered forests, and that are third-party certified. Malloy prints with soy and vegetable based inks, and over 98 percent of the solid material they discard is recycled. Their water emissions are entirely safe for disposal into their municipal sanitary sewer system, and they work with the Michigan Department of Environmental Quality to ensure that their air emissions meet all environmental standards.

The Michigan Department of Environmental Quality has recognized Malloy as a Great Printer for their compliance with environmental regulations, written environmental policy, pollution prevention efforts, and pledge to share best practices with other printers. Their county Department of Planning and Environment has designated them a Waste Knot Partner for their waste prevention and recycling programs.